C000277772

CAN WE GO TO LUNCH?

Winning, Developing, and Mentoring
the Heart of a Teenager

Kendra Berry & Kenya Sloan

Clay Bridges
PRESS

Can We Go to Lunch?

Winning, Developing, and Mentoring the Heart of a Teenager

eISBN: 978-1-68488-058-4
ISBN: 978-1-68488-057-7

Special Sales: Clay Bridges Press titles are available in special quantity discounts. Custom imprinting or excerpting can also be done to fit special needs. Contact Lucid Books at Info@claybridgespress.com

Mission

We want to encourage and equip
mentors of all types to love, invest, and
develop the people in their lives.
Everyone should have the opportunity
to be fully known and deeply loved.

Author Bios

Kendra

Through her experiences in youth development in public education, higher education, sports, non-profits, and faith-based organizations, Kendra has directly experienced how adults who are committed to mentoring students can positively impact the trajectory of their lives. Kendra began her career running operations for YMCA Teen Camp in Greenville, South Carolina. At her next stop in the athletic department at the University of Tennessee she worked in academic support, providing mentoring and guidance to multiple men's and women's teams. Kendra continued her work in education for the Community Schools strategy at the Knox Education Foundation by connecting educators, community, parents, and students to maximize growth and outcomes for all involved. Currently, Kendra works at Social Finance, a national impact finance and advisory nonprofit where they work with the public, private, and social sectors to create partnerships and investments to help people and communities realize improved outcomes in education, economic mobility, health, and housing. Outside of her professional career, Kendra has spent most of the last decade serving in student ministry as a small group leader and more recently in student ministry leadership at Faith Promise Church. Kendra is passionate about all young people having someone in their corner who is committed to knowing them fully, loving them deeply, and helping them grow and develop.

Author Bios

Kenya

Student-athlete and ministry leader are the roles that have marked most of Kenya's life up until this point. Through her positions on her teams and from the sport of wrestling, she has learned what it means to be a team player and intentionally encourage the people around her as well as how to work hard and learn to lean into discipline. Her roles in ministry have set her up to talk to, understand, and be compassionate towards all types of people. In the local churches she has been a member of, both in Tennessee and in Kentucky, she has been responsible for student volunteer teams, planning and facilitating gatherings and events, preparing for speaking engagements, etc. Kenya is also the co-author of *Can We Go to Lunch?* which documents the ways in which her life and future have been inspired and impacted through the means of a good friendship and intentional mentorship. Her hope is that by sharing the story of how her mentor was obedient to God and loved her well, other such relationships will be encouraged and thus impact the lives of teenagers exponentially.

Contact Information

Do you have a passion for developing people?
Do you believe mentoring well matters?
Do you believe in serving the next generation?
We would love to connect with you!

Website
canwegotolunch.com

Email
canwegotolunch@gmail.com

Social Media
Twitter: @canwegotolunch
Facebook: Can We Go To Lunch?
Instagram: @can_we_go_to_lunch

Table of Contents

Dedication

To every coach, teacher, mentor, parent, aftercare employee, student ministry volunteer and anyone who wants to win, develop, and mentor the heart of a teenager you love. Here is our story. We hope it intersects with your story, so we can all tell a story that shines bright in the darkness.

Foreword

"I have a dream." What did you first think when you read that? Most likely it was Rev. Martin Luther King Jr. and his "I Have A Dream" speech. Can you imagine leaving such a legacy -- that just a few words would inspire people for decades after they were spoken? It is not an over-exaggeration to say that I have a dream that student ministries, and the relationships they are built on, around the world would resemble this book! I have had the privilege to lead hundreds of leaders and thousands of students as our Global Student Pastor and I can tell you that this book is the archetype of what the coming generations need so desperately.

Do you ever wish there was more detailed information about how Jesus equipped and developed the disciples? Every time I read the gospels; I ask Jesus to download into me the things that are not on the pages. How did Jesus correct the disciples? How did He encourage them? How did Jesus put up with them?! I mean, being around 12 dudes 24/7 for three years would drive anyone crazy! In John 21:25 it says, "Jesus did many other things as well. If every one of them were written down, I suppose that even the whole world would not have room for the books that would be written." Just as the Holy Spirit guided the writers of the Bible, I truly believe there was a Holy Spirit download that guided the relationship recorded in the pages of this book to bring texture, prescription, and inspiration to the discipleship teenagers need today.

I watched the relationship between Kendra and Kenya unfold – it was intentional, powerful, and shifted the trajectory of both parties involved because of the relational and time investment made. Applying the content of this book will not be easy, but it will be worth it. It will not be short, but it will be worth it. It will not be clean cut, but it will be worth it. No matter your leadership level or religious beliefs, this book will educate, equip, and empower you to maximize mentorship and see it manifest the results you desire. This includes the teenagers in your life and the ones in your groups, communities, and organizations. This book applies a principle I have come to live by and that is this: time reveals truth. If you're willing and open to learning and adjusting your current practices and positions on mentorship, you too will see that this text is revealed as true as you apply the content to your own relationships.

For those of you that do believe in God, would you allow me to encourage you? As you take on the mantle that God has put on you of pursuing the coming generations, receive the mind-blowing truth that God has called you to it. Whatever He calls you to, you can trust He will bring you through. This text is an amazing tool that God will use to do just that.

Zac Stephens, Associate Senior Pastor
Faith Promise Church

Ground Rules

We cannot tell our story without Jesus, God, and the Kingdom. To take Him out would be a blow to the integrity of our story and make it woefully incomplete. If you are not on board with the Jesus thing just yet, we understand. And while we certainly wish you were, the truth is that there is power in following a principle whether you believe in its source or not. If you are kind, you can still reap the benefits of being kind, even if you do not believe in "do unto others as you would have them do unto you." You can still reap the benefits of friendships and relationships even if you do not necessarily believe in biblical community. You do not have to believe in raising up the next generation for the Lord, but you can still reap the benefits from pouring into kids and teenagers.

No matter where you and Jesus stand, we still believe that the principles that we walked through together have the ability to help facilitate the deep relationship that you desire with your teenager. Not only do we believe that these principles will help you win the heart of your teenager, but once you win their heart you will gain the permission and ability to speak into their lives and begin to help develop them into who they have been called to be.

Over the seven years of Kenya's teenage life, Kendra used specific principles to win and develop her heart. If we are being honest, we do hope that this helps other people who love teenagers, but we also wanted to capture our story. We have seen the power of our relationship in both of our lives and in the lives of the people around us. We never want to forget the details of how our relationship unfolded and what we learned along the way.

Most of the book is told from Kendra's viewpoint, with Kenya chiming in to explain what the effect really was and whether it worked as intended. Dive in and let us know if you find some insights into winning, developing, and mentoring the heart of a teenager.

Part I

Chapter 1

CAN WE GO TO LUNCH?

"I'm not a bang the table leader...getting my way by brute force...I am a set the table leader. Set the table leaders invite people to bring their best selves."

~*Dr. Krish Kandiah*

Sunday, January 28, 2018, Kenya's Senior Year
Can We Go To Lunch?

KENDRA
It was a regular Sunday. By this point in life we had established a Sunday routine. Church service at 10:00 a.m., front row, middle section on the right. Kenya always got the aisle seat. Corporate worship is a heartbeat that our

hearts share and know well. No matter where we were in the city and where we were in our schedules, some time on Saturday night I would check in. "Hey, what service are we sitting tomorrow?" More times than not, Kenya would choose the middle service. That Sunday in January was no different. Like every Sunday, I would show up early, to make sure we had seats. Worship would start, and she would come hustling in about halfway through the first song.

Internally, I always went back and forth between rolling my eyes because she was late and wanting to give her a hug because I would be so happy to see her. After service, we went about our ministry duties, development meeting or pastoral responsibilities for me and student ministry greeting for her. The rhythm of life was beautiful, and honestly one of my favorite things about our relationship: the fact that we did life together.

Around 1:00, the last service would end, people would flood to their cars and core volunteers and church staff would hang out. As someone who has intentionally loved, developed, mentored, and done life side by side with people for over a decade, I came to understand that this "after" time was intentionally and strategically orchestrated. That semester, Kenya had wrestling practice at 3:00 most Sundays, so there was a perfect window of time for creating a lunch opportunity.

Most Sundays, I planned ahead and thought through her schedule that led to the "Hey, what are you doin' the rest

4

of the day?" or a "You got plans for food?" I had created space in multiple ways in my life, schedule, and budget so on the chance that she would be free to spend some time together, I would be able to say yes.

This Sunday, though, was the middle of wrestling season. When you have a high school kid who is as talented as Kenya is, coming by free time in her schedule is hard. She is also an incredible person to be around, so I was not the only one who sought after her time. Everyone wanted to spend time with her.

So when she asked me the question that Sunday in January, the question we named the book after, my heart lit up.

"Can we go to lunch?" she said.

In that moment, I could have had several responses. There is no way I could have communicated everything then. How much I cared about her. How I move things around for her. "Can we go to lunch?" *Kid, you could ask me for the moon and I would try to get it for you. Lunch? That's nothing.* But I didn't say all of that. I had learned over the years that love is spelled T-I-M-E and that actions speak louder than words. So on that Sunday, in the rhythm of the life we did together, I told her, "Of course we can go to lunch." Huge smile on my face. Trying not to hug her again.

Who We Are

I can credit a big part of who I am, what I do, and my understanding of why to this woman. Now, Kendra did not make me who I am. Instead, she showed me how to understand and operate out of who I was created to be. This wasn't a coincidence and it definitely didn't happen by accident. What I recognize now (but was completely oblivious to eight years ago) is that there was divine instruction, intentionality, and great grace involved in her life's influence in mine.

There was divine instruction, much intentionality, and great grace involved in her life's influence in mine.

So, in telling our story, or at least some of what we can recall of doing life together over the past few years, we hope to not only share with you the joy we experience because of it, but also bring you in on some of the ways we are both better because of each other and what God has been doing with, through, and for us along the way.

I come from a rather small family. I've got three parents, my mom, my dad, and my stepmom, that love me more than I find justifiable. I've got a brother who is 11 months younger than me; he's been my best friend and partner in crime for literally longer than I can remember. My family is close, probably closer than most in our current society and culture. We support each other in everything, we love each other rather boundaryless, and we all have great pride to be a part of the family that we are a part of.

From a young age, my dad instilled his theory that if we, as young people, weren't busy, we were probably in trouble...so my brother and I both played sports. We played many of them growing up, but one stuck for the both of us: wrestling. It became our thing and eventually just became my thing. I started wrestling when I was around eight years old, did it through middle and high school and continue to do it now in college. I was also involved in an abundance of other activities in high school, clubs and volunteer positions and such. For me, high school was marked by *busyness*. For whatever reason though, it never felt like that. Now granted, there were a few things I did to make dad happy and a few things I did because I felt like it was my responsibility ...but for the most part, I did things, went places, and served in roles simply because I wanted to.

I know now that I am a VERY relational person, and it makes sense. I continued to wrestle even when I didn't want to because I couldn't let my coach down. A big part of the reason I served in positions at my church was because I enjoyed the people I served with. I joined clubs at my school because the adults involved believed in and wanted me on their team. When traced back to motive, for me, almost everything boils down to people. When I've got way too much energy than I know to do with, my go-to solution is community. When I'm in a funk and feel *bleh*, my go-to solution is community. When I'm confused or have questions, my go-to is community. People are my answer for just about everything. So, as you could imagine, I am immensely thankful for the people that I have in my life. Truly, I'm surrounded by the best of the best humans. From my immediate family, to my extended family, friends, mentors, teachers, coaches, and teammates…I've got the best and the crazy thing is, I rarely chose them!

I'm currently studying (please don't ask me what) and wrestling at a small private school in Kentucky called Campbellsville University. My life there looks a bit different than it did the previous 18 years, but there are plenty of consistencies. I still love people (the ones I do life with now just have different faces) and I still wrestle (which is still a love/hate relationship). I still do school, I still do relationships, and I still do church. How all of these things are done have changed and will continue to as I step into new and different seasons of life. But the foundation of who I am and the God who is beside and inside of me will not. Understanding these things has already proven immensely important in all areas of my life.

KENDRA
What you may not be able to tell from Kenya's introduction of herself is that when she walks into a room, the atmosphere changes. When she walks in, a smile walks in. And not to get hyper-religious, but because Jesus is fully and completely in her, when she walks in,

the Jesus in her walks in as well. The kid just radiates Him.

She has got qualities that parents only wish that their teenage kids had. She is polite and respectful to any and everyone around her. She is disciplined. Which is honestly part of how she became so accomplished. If I told you that in high school she was the only four-time state champion of girls wrestling in our state that would be pretty impressive. However, in addition to that, she left high school with a list of accolades and extracurriculars that could have earned her admission into the college of her choosing. The list included most charitable (voted on by classmates), the highest honor given to one senior in the senior class (voted on by faculty), Honor's Orchestra, Student Athlete Leadership Team, and a debutante…once again, just to name a few.

Through every event and award ceremony that year—and there were quite a few—I don't remember going to anything and not seeing her get awarded for something. As someone who knew and had walked with her for a few years, I knew it was all deserving, and I was excited that she was being recognized as a result of her hard work.

I have known since I was little that I loved kids. As a teenager, I could not have told you what that meant for my career, but as I got older, I realized that I have been wired to love and develop people. And while I thought that it was only teenagers, what I've learned is that it has really been my job to reach back to those I may be a few seasons in front of and love them well. Just like those in front of me did for me.

The relationship that Kenya and I developed occurred outside of my professional career, but what I tell people is that kids are the bulk of my life. It doesn't matter if that means younger kids (my nephew, niece and godkids currently range from 4 to 10); older kids (I work at a middle school where kids span 11 to 14); or teenagers at church like Kenya who were anywhere from 12 to 18. I was lucky to have people who stewarded me well and helped me clearly understand that God has called me to the next generation.

Professionally, I have a few degrees and there are letters after my name, but I actually found Kenya to be a much better teacher. Probably the most impactful thing I took from graduate school was when I left. With a door closed to pursue a PhD, I had a choice. Fight a decision that had been made, or trust God and step into the next season He had for me. It was a tormentingly difficult decision for me, the recovering perfectionist, and the brave choice was to admit that this season was done (at least for now) and walk away.

As I reflect, I realize that the timing of my choice aligned with Kenya stepping into her last two years of high school. The Lord did not want me doing dissertation research on teenagers I did not know. He wanted to provide ample time to develop a relationship with the one teenager who was most important to me. My season transitioning from graduate school into a full-time job freed up my time to pour my life into hers.

You know it is ironic, I knew when I started that PhD program that something was not right. In every class it felt like a game of "one of these is not like the other." Everyone would propose these ideas and I would shoot them down as I explained why that would not work in real life with an actual teenager. I thought I needed "Dr." in front of my name. But why? For legitimacy? To feel important? To feel accomplished? To check another box? Probably some piece of all of those. Instead, God gave me a greater gift. He gave me Kenya.

> *Jesus taught me what it meant to have influence, true influence, in someone's life. And that's what is truly important.*

Now I believe in research and I believe in data, but in my heart, I am a practitioner, and what Kenya and I learned together came from first-person experience data collecting. I thought I needed to appear important. Instead, Jesus taught me what it meant to have influence, true influence, in someone's life. And that's what is truly important. Which leads us to our first principle.

Chapter 2

WHO YOU ARE IS MORE IMPORTANT THAN WHAT YOU DO

"His approval addiction didn't just play itself out relationally, it played itself out professionally. Here he is doing his job. He's accomplished, he's busy, he's booked. But the grind was an indication of an infection from rejection. What's impressive is not 'Can you grind? What's impressive is 'Can you stop?'"

~Dharius Daniels

I would have to write another book to be able to walk you through all of Kenya's accomplishments. And while I tell you them to give some context, the truth is that most of our time together was spent outside of the context of these accomplishments. Now of course I went to the tournaments, and performances, and award ceremonies. I think it is important to show up for these things. However, the majority of our time was spent around the person she was becoming, not the things she was doing.

I knew that what she chose to do with her life would change over time based on the season she was in. But the core of who she is, who the Lord created her to be, needed to be nailed down and firmly cemented.

> *The majority of our time was spent around the person she was becoming, not the things she was doing.*

I always told her that the Lord wired and uniquely created her to love people well. For those of us who follow Christ, we know that we have all been commanded to love. When I learned that important parts of the Bible are wrapped up in the phrase "Love God, love people," I got really excited because I cannot do a lot of things right, but that I do well.

Also as Christians, let's be honest, we don't genuinely like everyone, but we have been called to love everyone and some people do it better than others. I laugh a little when people tell me that I love others well. I shake my head and smile, because I think *there's a reason for that. I love because we have been commanded to.* Kenya, on the other hand…it's just different. Where most of us have to work to love those we do not particularly like (you have someone in mind, don't you!), she just seems to do it naturally.

Kenya is set apart in ways that I will never be able to fully understand. But I think the combination of how well she loves, how she genuinely and consistently tries to grow in Jesus, the influence she carries...it all led the Holy Spirit to tap me on the shoulder when she was 13 and tell me that she was the kid I was going to pour into in my next season of life. It all started, ironically if you know her well, with football.

Fall 2012, Kenya's 7th grade year
Back to the Beginning

KENYA

I totally wish I could tell you exactly when my story and Kendra's story intersected. But I can't. Not because it's a secret or anything… merely because I, for the life of me, cannot remember. It actually wasn't until we were talking about the details of this book, that I even realized the first time we met. Kendra mentioned some football playing in our church parking lot. Sounds about right.

What I do know is that Kendra and I found ourselves in the same student ministry in a church in my hometown of Knoxville, Tennessee, though we played very different roles there at the time. Kendra was THE loudest, most outgoing, energy filled middle school small group leader. She led middle school girls, but she did more than that. I remember seeing her everywhere—or so it seemed. Kendra was the type of person who was just there to make sure the people around her had what they needed and that every human in the room felt as comfortable and welcome as possible. In the lobby of our church, Kendra probably skipped more than she walked, jumped more than she stood still, and laughed more than she actually said words. Though, as you will learn, there was so much more Kendra offered...but to me, at the time, she was the energy box that had to be present at any and all student ministry gatherings and events. I, on the other hand, was the extremely curious, extremely timid middle school girl just trying to hide in the crowd.

It was a random Wednesday night in the summer between my 6th and 7th grade year that my brother and I moseyed into the big church on the highway a few minutes from my house. I had no idea what I was doing there. Didn't for months. I didn't have any friends that went there. My brother found friends quickly, so he didn't hang around with me long. I grew up in church but hadn't completely bought into the whole Jesus thing yet. But Faith Promise Students (FpStudents), as we were called, felt like a safe place. And they had cool lights. Soooooo...yeah. I showed up week after week, not really looking to be seen or heard. I just liked to listen and observe.

My first actual memory I recall having with Kendra wasn't until I'd been in the ministry at this church for over a year! What?! I know. Crazy right? How in the world can Kendra recall the very first time we met (and probably many details after that), and my brain has stored no significant memory of interaction with this woman until almost a year later? I think the answer is quite simple; in fact, it rather clearly demonstrates the nature of our relationship. From day one, Kendra was intentional in her thoughts, words, and actions towards me. She was on assignment. All the while, in my eyes, I'm just this random girl in the mix of hundreds of middle and high school students. And Kendra is just this random leader that I've had a few conversations with in the mix of all the others in this massive ministry. For me, there was not much of a connection...until summer camp at Johnson Bible college.

KENDRA
Kenya and I met in the student ministry we were a part of, FpStudents, in Knoxville, Tennessee. As a 24-year-old who loved teenagers and who loved Jesus, student ministry was the place for me. I was young and energetic, so they put me with middle school girls. In those first few years, even though Kenya was a 7th grader, she was not in my group; I was given other girls to shepherd and develop in that season.

One of the things that characterizes our student ministry is fun. With it being fall we would have planned a series of tailgate/football style activities outside. Throwing the football and Frisbees, bonfire going once it got dark, those kinds of things. Not exactly the "girly" kind of stuff.

I am not nor have I ever been the Disney princess, pink shirts, flowers, baby doll kind of girl. Not as a little girl and definitely not as an adult. I have always gravitated towards sports, K'nex, electronics, and books. By age 24, my college basketball days were only two years behind me, and this meant that I still told myself two things, both of which may or may not have been true: One: I'm still athletic. Two: I still got it. Which meant that I was out there playing football with a group of mainly high school boys. Although my skill at throwing a football has always been below the expectation I have for myself, there are very few times in my life where my coordination and athleticism fail me and that includes parking lot football.

Here enters Kenya into the football fun and into my life. The reality is that we are most often drawn to people who are like us in some way. Even though "opposites attract" is a popular saying, I'll tell you like my uncle told me at the age of 12: "You better find someone who has the same values as you." The first thing that stood out to me about Kenya was the fact that she looked like me. Not deeply insightful or helpful, but I'm just being honest. Living in east Tennessee, specifically Knoxville, where well over 70% of the population is white, the number of people who look like me is nowhere near the number of those who do not. And our church and student ministry followed a similar pattern. The other obvious thing that I noticed was that she was a girl. We are out here, in the fall, with the sun setting, playing football and there are not too many girls out here...and yet here she is. Not only that, but she is pretty athletic. My kind of person. I probably made the decision right then that she would be someone I could connect with.

Who You Are Is More Important Than What You Do
As we got to know each other over the years, I saw that Kenya did a lot of things extremely well. By her senior year, she was speaking at her high school graduation, winning the highest award given to a member of her graduating class, and headed off to wrestle at the collegiate level. However, one of the things I always wanted to make sure she understood was that I was only slightly concerned with what she was *doing* and incredibly more concerned with who she was *becoming*.

That meant my mentoring needed to align with this priority. For starters, I tried and still try diligently to never start a conversation by asking her about school. Now hear me out: I am a huge fan of education. All four of my grandparents were educators. I was 27 by the time I was no longer enrolled in school. I also work for a non-profit in a public school. However, at no point did I want her to believe that her grades were the most important thing about her, because they were not. We talked about school, and I gave my feedback when I was asked about classes and college, but it was always in context and I tried to let her determine the right time and place for these conversations to occur.

For the majority of Kenya's high school years, her main extracurricular was wrestling. And saying she was good was an understatement. I mean, the girl won the state championship four times and her high school record was 87-0. She was really, really good. And while we talked about wrestling, it was much more about the intangible things around it—attitude, how she was influencing other people—as opposed to how much she won.

We talked about how when she prepped for a match she worshipped and reminded herself who she was in God, not who she was in wrestling, and how this was a key part of her warm-up. We talked about the importance of her being a good teammate. How wrestling was one avenue to love the people in her circle well and a chance to dive into their lives on a personal level. We talked about how she had been gifted with leadership and influence and how she was going to steward those gifts with the time she had been given. Wrestling was what she was "doing," but developing her identity, being a good teammate, stewarding leadership well—these were things that she would not only take into her next season, but would also follow her long after her wrestling career had finished.

As you mentor teens, it is critical that you be aware of what you are communicating. If someone were to ask your teen what you believe is most important about them, what would they say? Would it be their grades? Is that the first thing you always ask them about? Is it the thing you are most angry about when it does not go well? Is it sports? Are their practices, trainings, and game schedules your main focus? Is their continuous improvement in this area communicated more than the fact that you love them? Do they know you believe they have value outside of the sport that they play? Is it performing? Have you communicated that everything in their lives is dependent on the next audition or recital? Do you act as if life is over when they do not succeed the way you would have hoped? What are we communicating to our teenagers?

I submit to you that who they are is *worlds* more important than what they do. What they do will change over time, a number of times. However, the core of who they are, how they see the world, how they see themselves—that is the space that we want to earn the right to speak into. That is where your effort and time is best spent.

Chapter 2 Reflection Questions:

1. Which do you celebrate more: your teenager's accomplishments or their character?
2. Which parts of their character do you discuss with them?
3. Which parts of their character do they need to work on?
4. Which parts of your character do you model well?
5. Which parts of your character do you need to work on?

_____

_____

_____

_____

_____

_____

_____

_____

_____

_____

_____

_____

_____

_____

_____

Chapter 3

DO LIFE TOGETHER

"It will be the people with the greatest love, not the most information, who influence us to change."

~Bob Goff

Fall 2014, Kenya's 9th grade year
This Kid is Legit

By the time Kenya had reached her freshman year, Jesus had already tapped me on the shoulder and told me that she was my assignment that season. Well, to be honest, I thought I was assigned to *her*. You know, to help her grow and develop and whatnot. Maybe that was part of it, but the reality is that God gave her to *me* to fill, grow, and develop *me*. By the Fall of 2014, she was a freshman in high school, and I was no longer leading a small group but coaching a group of adults who were working with and leading all of the 9th grade girls at our church.

This was actually before I got to know Kenya well. This new role gave me plenty of time to watch, learn, and observe who Kenya was. It gave me a reason to step into their conversations and take an interest in her small group.

After small group time at our church one night, Kenya and a student came bounding down the stairs, Bible open. Kenya made a beeline for me. Honestly, I do not remember the question that she asked. Clearly they had an incredible small group that got them talking and thinking about the things of God. In that moment, though, I did not have the answer. But I didn't panic. I understood something we always train our small group leaders on: you do not have to have all the answers to your teens' questions. All I had in the moment was: "That's a great question. Let's go find our student pastor."

Even though I cannot remember what she asked me, I do remember being impressed by the question she asked and how far past "surface level" she was willing to go. I also remember her demeanor. She was excited to learn about the Word. Excited to get a revelation from Jesus. I had noticed her because she stood out, but that was one of the solidifying moments where I distinctly remember that something was different about her.

I think one of the special things that Kenya has done for me over the years is hold me accountable like no one else ever had. I know that I will have to stand and give an account before God of how I have stewarded all that He has given me. Not just money and things, but more importantly, that means people. I close my eyes and imagine the Lord asking me "I entrusted you with Kenya, how did you honor that?" And I will have to give an account for what I shared with her. So when the theological question from Scripture came…then was not the time to make something up. Then was not the time to try and fudge it. Because if I were to knowingly inaccurately communicate or interpret the Word, that is something for which I would be accountable to our heavenly Father. "I don't know" is a much better option than just winging it.

What they want is your time. What they want is the real you.

For anyone trying to develop a teenager's heart, one thing that you cannot substitute is time. Time cannot be replaced by money, or things, or a strong desire for them to succeed. The relationship between Kenya and I grew so strong in part because I saw her at least twice a week for 6 years. From 7th to 12th grade I was able to make small, consistent, spiritual, and very human deposits every week.

Then there was the showing up for events like wrestling matches and orchestra concerts, the "come over for dinner" and "let's hang out on the couch" time. I didn't have to be "cool" like them. That's not what they're looking for. What they want is your time. What they want is the real you. No matter what you are trying to communicate, no matter what you want them to believe, you need to consistently deposit it over time.

Even though our relationship began in student ministry, I always thought it was interesting that I was never Kenya's small group leader. The more I think about that, I am grateful. I think that it was much more meaningful that we chose to pursue this mentoring relationship with each other even when we did not have to. Had I been her small group leader, there may have always been the lingering thought that I was mentoring her because I *had* to. It was always important to me for that string not to be attached. I never wanted her to have a reason to question my motives. I never wanted to leave space for doubt to creep in. It was not until her junior/senior year that she technically "reported" to me in her serving role in our student ministry, but by then our relationship had been created and solidified.

Do Life Together

The sheer amount of time Kenya and I spent together over the years enabled us to do a few things. First, and perhaps most obvious, we got to know each other extremely well. From inside jokes, to knowing looks from across the room, to the other one finding the word that was on the tip of the other's tongue. There are intricacies that are developed purely because of time. Jada Edwards, an experienced Bible teacher and mentor, says that intimacy comes from character and consistency. Kenya and I were indeed consistent over an extended period of time.

Second, by spending time together we got to know the people who were closest to each of us. Parents know the importance of knowing their teenager's friends. The fact that who we are is a result of the people we spend the most time with is not a new statement. As I spent time with Kenya, I wanted to get to know her friends and those she spent the most time with. This is because, as someone who loved her, I needed to know who was pouring into her when I was not around—and what they were pouring.

I knew that when Kenya spent time with me, she heard messages such as *I believe in you* and *I am so proud of how you love other people.* However, I needed to know what the other people in her life spoke into her as well. So I intentionally put myself in Kenya and her friends' path. I positioned myself so I could be invited for dinner when parents were cooking, so I could be invited to late night ice cream runs when they left church on a Wednesday, so I could be invited over for birthday parties, and celebrations, and routine trips to the grocery store. Because I wanted to make sure that she was hearing and internalizing messages that were all moving and encouraging her in the same direction.

Subsequently, she got to know my people. The friends I did ministry with, the mentors and families who poured into me, and my parents were all people that she got to know over time. I wanted to expose Kenya to all of these incredible people who had helped shape me into the person that she knew. A lot of the things I said and did with her were because people had said and done those things with me. I wanted her to have direct access to the most influential people in my life.

Once you begin to know someone that well, two things happen. One, you have put in enough consistent time that you can see their blind spots, the areas they can't see about themselves but that others can, and two, you earn the right to point them out. One without the other will not do. If you spend a significant amount of time where you can see your mentee's blind spots, but you do not have a good relationship with them, then calling out their blind spots is going to do more harm than good. Think about it, how well do you do with the people who criticize you, but don't have a good relationship with you? Probably not so well.

Criticism outside of the context of relationship rarely goes well, especially for teenagers. For teenagers, this is personal: until you have earned the right to speak into particular parts of their lives, you must tread carefully. Not earning that right can be dangerous and cost you your credibility in the relationship.

I had this happen to me before.

In one season, I had a friend who had spent a lot of time with me and had earned the right to call out my blind spots. However, as we got older and our lives went their separate ways, we no longer spent nearly as much time together as we originally did. Years later, when she went to call out a blind spot and she was completely off, I did not receive it well. I was hurt that even though she had earned the right to speak into me in the past, in that current season she had not spent as much time with me to get the blind spots right. That friend lost credibility with me that day because she was so off-base.

The last advantage to spending significant time with your teen mentee is that it enables you to get to know their heart so well that you can pick up where you left off after large amounts of time away from each other (weeks or months, not years). Like most relationships, Kenya's and mine did not happen in a bubble. We both had large commitments such as school, church, and community. We both also had significant relationships with other people. Combine this with the fact that she was one of the best female wrestlers in the country and there would be stretches where we would not see each other for weeks at a time. When she left for college this turned into months at a time where I did not see her. As the amount of time we spent together decreased, I wondered at times how it would affect our mentoring relationship.

What I know now that I did not know then was that we had built such a foundation in our relationship that we really knew each other's heart. So when months would pass by between Fall break and Christmas break, and when she would come home for the summer, what I came to realize is that we had spent so much time together that we could pick up right where we left off.

That does not mean that we had not grown and changed in those months; however, the core of who we were had not. The fundamental principles that we believed had not changed.

Chapter 3 Reflection Questions:
1. Do you spend consistent time with your teenager?
2. How do you spend structured time together?
3. How can you spend unstructured time together?

_____

_____

_____

_____

_____

_____

_____

_____

_____

_____

_____

_____

_____

_____

Chapter 4

DECIDE HOW MUCH YOU LOVE THEM

"How can you let yourself be loved if you can't let yourself be seen? Vulnerability is the path back to each other, but we are so afraid to get on it."

~*Brene Brown*

Fast Forward-Summer 2019

KENYA

I was looking forward to this day. Kendra had a surprise excursion planned. I don't handle surprises well, so I made sure she was very sure of her decision not to inform me of where we were going that day. I asked, I tried to guess, but she wouldn't budge.

I remember the long drive to the river. I got out of the car to witness acres and acres of sunflowers! Kendra knew I loved them. But in between my thoughts of and appreciation for the day's surprise, my brain was heavy with a single looming thought. It was about a ball that I had dropped. It was a conversation that I'd hoped wouldn't come up.

Earlier that week I was supposed to have completed some writing for this book. I'm not a super-punctual, organized person, if you catch my drift. But Kendra had planned out a very clear writing schedule for the both of us, as well as a way to track it with milestones. We had talked about it, confirmed that it was reasonable, checked in on progress several times, and when the day came for me to meet one of the biggest deadlines yet—I was far from finished.

This isn't new for me. I'm the type of student who turns their assignments in online at 11:59 p.m. the night they're due and finishes their class presentations on her way to class. I cut it close frequently and when it comes to timelines, I miss and ask for forgiveness often. This was, however, very new to Kendra. It never occurred to me that she'd never had to deal with me in this manner before. And alike, I had never been responsible to her for much, especially anything with a structured timeline.

In this process I wasn't concerned much—until the deadline had passed. The conversation I knew I had to have with Kendra felt really heavy in comparison to the ones I'd had with my parents or my professors or my work supervisors. This mattered a lot to someone that I cared about a lot, and I didn't know how she'd respond. I was scared that she would be upset with me, or hurt, or disappointed…so I avoided the issue completely. I avoided all relevant topics— deadlines or responsibilities or writing or books—so hard that it felt obvious and awkward.

So as we walked and oohed and awed at the stunning beauty of God's creation, I thought hard about the conversation to be had and the fact that we weren't having it. The same was true as we ate at my favorite restaurant. And the same was true as we chatted it up with our friends at church that night. In fact, the issue was so heavy on my mind and heart that the moment a mutual friend asked how I was doing (and Kendra was NOT in ear shot) I confessed what was overwhelming me. I spilled the beans. Told her what I'd been keeping in all day. "I missed a deadline that Kendra set and I'm avoiding the issue on purpose. She seems fine, but I'm scared to know how she feels about it. I let her down and there is nothing I can do at this point to fix it."

Finally, on the car ride home, the elephant was addressed. Kendra brought it up. I didn't say much. I knew now wasn't the time to justify why I'd messed up. I needed only to listen, understand, own up, and apologize. But come to find, I owed her two apologies. Yes, one for dropping the ball, which hurt her more than it disappointed her. But two, for running so hard. Kendra reminded me of what I already knew.

"We don't do that," she said. "We talk about the hard things; we don't ignore them." And she was right. How much easier it would have been, how much more I would have enjoyed our day together, how much more honor I would have shown her, if we'd just done the thing from the get-go. Bringing up how I felt, where I messed up, what scared me, and why was the hard thing but the best thing. What was cool is that we got there anyway...because of Kendra. When I couldn't share my heart about the topic, she shared hers. She opened the can, told me how I made her feel and…boom! Issue addressed. Not fixed immediately, but it definitely put us on the same page for the future. I appreciated her because I knew how hard it was. Sharing my heart was what I'd been struggling to do our entire day we were together. I learned that being vulnerable and honest isn't easy, but with the people you love and care about, it is immensely worth it.

> *"We talk about the hard things; we don't ignore them."*

KENDRA

What has been interesting is how much the two of us have learned throughout this book writing process. Not only about the process of book writing, but also about each other. During the summer of 2019 we were in the thick of trying to put together some of the main content for the book. Now for me that means a strict writing schedule so we could stay on track and pace out how we are going to finish. For Kenya that means a little bit more of "we'll figure it out."

Now if this sounds like a bit of a difference or a bit of conflict, you would be 100% correct! I tend to treat a deadline like it is written in stone, and Kenya's treatment of a deadline can at times be...flexible. So the day before we were scheduled to spend the better part of the day together, I had set an internal writing deadline for us and she missed it. Now in the grand scheme of life, it truly was not that big of a deal. After all, you are reading this book.

Now that she is in college in a different state, our time together is precious, and we want to always be intentional. In the last few days that we both had free that summer, we had a great plan to spend the day together. We went and saw the sunflowers down by the river. Hundreds of acres of sunflowers, gently swaying in the sun. We walked up and down rows upon rows of them and took pictures with the beautiful bright blue sky contrasting on their bright yellow, happy blooms. We walked along the river and sat on the hand-carved bench that someone had donated, talking about things that matter.

We then went to dinner at O'Charley's. It was free pie Wednesday, and the rolls are good every time!

After dinner, we headed to hang out with our student ministry at church. It's always fun for me when she comes back. There are people who are so excited to see her. She had and has so many key relationships in her life there. It is not only where we met, but where we shared so much. It is always fun to stand there and listen to her update everyone on how things are going, ask great questions and re-ignite connections with friends and adults alike.

As we were in the thick of the writing process, we had begun to tell a handful of people here and there what we were working on. With our differences in how we approach deadlines fresh on my mind, I told a friend how Kenya and I had a mix-up earlier that week, just in passing. As I floated off to talk to another friend, I glanced back and saw that Kenya was talking to the same friend. As I went back to chat with both of them, I realized that Kenya and I had both separately told this friend of our deadline mix-up, but we had yet to talk about it.

I had intentionally not had the conversation yet that day because I did not want the tone of our day to be marked by a potentially difficult conversation. After all, I think deadlines are important, but I did not want the book writing process to negatively impact our mentoring relationship which had now turned into a friendship. So I figured if it came up naturally, then we would talk about it, and if not, I would be sure to address it by the end of the day.

Well, after late night worship we were finally headed home and after spending the day with her, the time had arrived for a tough conversation. What made it tough on my end was not the holding her accountable part, but the realization that I was going to have to be vulnerable and honest.

Now in hindsight, I chickened out a little, waiting until the 20-minute drive home to have the talk. This way, my eyes would need to be on the road. I wouldn't have to look at her. As we had this conversation, I remember the promise I made to be completely vulnerable. Most of the time that meant putting stuff out there and not knowing exactly how it was going to be received.

So with my classic Type One self (according to the Enneagram Institute, that means the Rational/Idealist: Principled, Purposeful, Self-Controlled, and Perfectionistic), I talked about how it is not only the way logistics, deadlines, and order helped me make sense of the world, but also how it made me feel unimportant and as if my priorities were not a priority to her. Those words are a lot easier to type now than they were to talk about in the moment.

Decide How Much You Love Them
My interpretation of the Bible was not the only place where Kenya held me accountable. What was more prevalent, day in and day out, was how she taught me what it means to love someone enough to be honest. Around her 11th grade year I remember making an intentional decision. I'm going to give Kenya my total commitment as a mentor.

That meant quite a few things. It meant that first, I was going to love her enough to be honest. Really honest. So she understands that as "the adult," I do not always have the answers and that I am not always going to get it right. I have flaws. The power struggle is so apparent in most relationships between adults and teenagers. Imagine the last conflict that you had with a teenager. Was there an element of convincing a teenager that you were right? Or getting them to do what you wanted? I am not saying that we cannot push them to be their best or hold them accountable, but if the relationship's primary basis is conflict, I do not think that gets people to where they want to be. I challenge you, as the adult, have the courage to disengage from the power struggle and be honest. It may get you further than you think.

Second, it meant that I was going to love her enough to be vulnerable and let her all the way in. Did a cringing feeling just come over you? Then you know exactly what I mean. As people who love Jesus, we are called to love everyone, and I try; however I am incredibly selective about who I let in. Like most people, I imagine that I am trying to protect myself from being hurt. If people don't know the real Kendra, then it is hard to hurt the real Kendra. The problem is that when we try and protect ourselves by not letting anyone in, we miss out on the joy of letting the right people in. In the book of Proverbs when it talks about guarding your heart, it does not say build a wall and let no one in. That is the wrong imagery. Instead, I imagine it should function more as a drawbridge that is protecting a castle with a moat. The purpose of the drawbridge is to let the right people in who are supposed to have access.

When you become so accustomed to keeping everyone out, you become numb to how much energy and effort it takes always having your guard up...

I wanted that. I wanted the chance to let the right people in. When you become so accustomed to keeping everyone out, you become numb to how much energy and effort it takes always having your guard up, ensuring that people only see exactly what you want them to see.

A chance to truly know someone and be truly known by someone: it was too good to pass up.

Third, I would have to share my heart and dreams. I once heard T.D. Jakes say that your dreams should be so big that you have to be careful who you tell them to. I had dreams that were much bigger than my eyes in my 20s. About the kind of family I wanted to have one day and how I thought Jesus wanted me to play a part in bringing heaven to earth. The things that are hard to say out loud. The things that if told to the wrong people stops the momentum that you have in your heart. I wanted to share Kingdom dreams with someone who cared about the Kingdom. I wanted to share my heart about the brokenness in our world that kept me up at night. You don't just do that with anyone.

I wish I had a specific example I could point to or a specific story to illustrate this, but the reality is that I made a conscious decision daily to let Kenya in and not keep her in the dark. Perhaps most importantly, I wanted to make sure she had a model of what it means to love wholeheartedly. I wanted to make sure that she knew what a healthy friendship looked like. I wanted to make sure she knew what it meant to be nervous to tell someone something, but have more trust in the person than fear of them having the information. She needed to see me push through discomfort. She needed to see me make intentional decisions about the big moments in my life. How much did I love her? Did I love her enough to model it for her? I hope I did. I hope I still do.

Chapter 4 Reflection Questions:
1. How honest have you been with your teenager about your struggles and faults?
2. Do they have reason to believe that you lead a perfect life?
3. How can you model vulnerability with them?

_____

_____

_____

_____

_____

_____

_____

_____

_____

_____

_____

_____

_____

_____

_____

Chapter 5

KINGDOM FAMILY

"There is one thing I can promise about destiny . . . you will not arrive by yourself . . . you're gonna need other people."

~Ron Carpenter

Summer 2015, Summer before Kenya's 10th grade year
Student Ministry Camp, Johnson University

KENYA
Movement Conference! Ahhhhh!

Movement is the name for the summer camp/conference our student ministry did every July. Each year it looked a little different, especially in the developing years of the camp, but two things that I could bank on as constants: fun and Jesus. I looked forward to this camp more than anything else. And this one would fall at the time that I was finally beginning to feel comfortable with the people around me at church (i.e. the girls in my small group and my small group leader). I was coming out of my shell! By this time, I guess I knew Kendra on a slightly more personal level than "that lady with a lot of energy at FpStudents," but we by no means had a really close relationship at this point. This week's camp was a major turning point in this regard.

It was here that I first remember Kendra really *being* there. Maybe it was day two or three of camp. It was night time, and while all the other kids were playing a bunch of fun, laughter-filled, messy games on the soccer field, I found myself on the sidelines: fallen on my knees, facing the empty sky, having the first vivid conversation with God that I can remember ever having. A few minutes into this heart to heart, Kendra enters the scene. I remember seeing her, on her knees, to my right. Far enough away to where I didn't feel like she was invading my moment, but close enough so that I knew she was there. She could have been there for quite some time, or she could have just rolled up when I noticed her there...I have no idea.

Kendra began to pray for me aloud. She prayed for several things as I remember. But to this day, the only words that I recall honing in on were, "God, would you send Kenya some friends?"

Immediately, I was offended. Deeply. "Why in the world is this lady that I barely know asking for God to send me friends? I mean, I know I don't really have any. I guess it's a bit more obvious than I thought. But. I'm completely fine without friends. I've never really had any, but I've always been just fine. I don't need God to send me any friends. She doesn't even know me."

Boy, was I wrong on several accounts! Kendra might not have known me all that well through experience, but she a) had a very intimate relationship with the God who knows me better than I know myself and b) paid attention.

Kendra might have noticed that I didn't have any particularly meaningful relationships, but I feel certain there was more to it. She knew things that I didn't, among which was the knowledge that community was oh-so-important. And not only did she observe that I didn't have much community, but she also must have had great concern because she knew that I was missing out on something that would be good for me. Community and relationship were things that I needed. She knew this to be true. And she cared. Wow.

KENDRA
Like many other student ministries, ours did a big camp or conference over the summer. While in the past we had gone far out of town to the beach or to a campground, that year we went to Johnson University, a small Bible college about 30 minutes from Knoxville. On one of the first

nights we were having free time outside: lawn games, soccer, ice cream, hanging out. It was a great relaxed atmosphere as the sun went down. As games were starting to wrap up, I was in 100% supervision mode, always scanning the crowd, making sure kids were where they were supposed to be, doing what they were supposed to be doing. I believe in the next generation like never before, but folks, teenagers are teenagers and we still watch them pretty closely.

As people were picking up supplies and others were lingering, I noticed Kenya sitting by herself at the far side of the ridge. I'm not talking like on the edge of where people are. She was across the gigantic field at least two soccer field lengths separate and apart from everyone else. I knew enough about Kenya at this point to know that this was out of character. There were always people around her and Jesus shining through her to others is the norm. So I walked across that field, gave a couple of feet between the two of us and sat down. In silence.

I did not know what was going on, and this was not a situation where I needed to just come out and ask. Our deeper relationship had not really started yet and at this point the goal was to 1) not scare her away, 2) get her talking, and 3) help any way I could. As we sat there in silence, after a while, I just did what I knew. After all, this was student ministry camp. I figured I would just pray. She was hurting, and in that moment that was the only answer that I had. I remember praying friends into her life, which makes sense because she was sitting by herself, but that was not the whole story. She is someone who loves wholeheartedly and genuinely enjoys and is energized by people. I had noticed that she always had people around her, but she had not quite found her squad yet. I thought it would mean a lot for her to have that. So I just prayed that Jesus would send her the people. The people in her life who were friends like family. People she could trust. People she did life with. Classmates who she had a deep connection with outside of school. We prayed the important things. I don't think I had the language at the time, but what I was really praying for was that Jesus would bring her a Kingdom Family.

Kingdom Family

We are the average of the five people we spend the most time with.

This is not an original thought. Every parent who has had concerns about their teenager's friends can attest to this. Who you spend your time with has a significant influence on your life. In culture, this is always framed as a negative for teenagers. "Be careful of who your kids hang out with…because you don't want them to drink or do drugs." And while this is true, I believe this is a limited mindset.

We do not only want them to not be around the wrong influences. We also want them to be around life-giving influences. As much as I love Kenya and as much time as I intentionally spent with her, I think that what I instinctively knew that day at summer camp was that there is something uniquely designed and valuable about having a family. And if it operates like the Kingdom of God does...then *whoa baby*, watch out.

We do not only want them to not be around the wrong influences. We also want them to be around life-giving influences.

By then I had been walking in the first few years of what my Kingdom family looked like. Other believers that I did life with. Where the only blood we had in common was the blood that Jesus spilled on a cross. However, this began to plant something in my heart all those years ago that is still true today, and that is that Kingdom Family is the best kind of family. Over the years, Kingdom Family fed me dinner, put air in my tires, lifted my soul, provided me a safe place, challenged my thinking and beliefs, supported my efforts to grow, encouraged my dreams...and gave me this overwhelming sense that "this is what it's supposed to be like."

Every teenager needs friends and people who can help create this kind of environment for them. There is more research out there than I can comprehend on how important peer influences are on teenagers. I did not just want Kenya to have good friends. I wanted more for her, and I hope you want more for your teenager. I wanted her to have a Kingdom Family; her tribe, her crew, her squad.

In the subsequent years, the Lord sent people. Friends that she met through school that became friends outside of school. Girls who could talk for hours about life and the future. The Lord also created the coolest brotherhood band around her that I've seen. As the only girl on her high school wrestling team, I saw them step up for her time and time again. I saw the Lord form her small group and give her a small group leader at church to where they had the tough conversations and discussed the hard things about Jesus that took longer than merely one conversation.

The Lord sent her people. He is such a faithful God.

Chapter 5 Reflection Questions:

1. Do you know the names of your teenager's friends?
2. Have you spent any time with your teenager's friends?
3. Does your teenager know who your close friends are?
4. What qualities do your friends model for your teenager?

_____

_____

_____

_____

_____

_____

_____

_____

_____

_____

_____

_____

_____

_____

_____

Chapter 6

WHAT YOU SAY NO TO DETERMINES WHAT YOU SAY YES TO

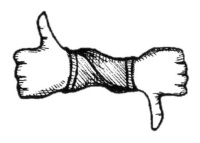

"You gotta know when you're wearing yourself out swinging at stuff that's not yours to fight…the peace of another person is not your responsibility. Your peace is your responsibility. There comes a point where you have to say that's not my battle."

~*Steven Furtick*

Fall 2016, Kenya's 11th grade year
Where is your time going?

KENYA

One Sunday morning, at some point between or after our routine responsibilities for that day, Kendra pulls me aside and we begin walking away from the busyness that is church on Sunday morning and towards the student administrative offices in the back. This wasn't an abnormal route for our walk-and-talks, but this time Kendra walks straight into the empty office that belongs to our global student pastor and holds the door open for me to walk in. Immediately I knew she had something planned. At first, I assumed we might be talking about ministry—the lack of enough volunteers for one of my teams, the miscommunication taking place between myself and some other student leaders, my unhealthily hectic Wednesday night routine, something. I have no idea why this was my immediate thought; our talks rarely centered around such things. Kendra was always encouraging and challenging me to think about me—the things that make me *me*, things that bring me joy, things that bother me, people that are important to me, things that make me better, etc. And that's what we did.

Time management is a skill that I've always managed to convince myself that I am much better at than I actually am. I didn't fully understand the significance of managing my time until I found myself in a spot in which I didn't have a choice but to do it and do it well. I vividly recall this Sunday morning when Kendra had decided enough was enough. I had probably mentioned being way too busy than I preferred and not feeling like I was in control of my time only 100 too many times.

We went into the office and she sat me in front of the enormous white board on the wall. After a brief preface of our goal and agenda for this time, Kendra proceeds to draw a diagram (that takes up the ENTIRE 3x5-foot white board) to help me break down how I generally spent the hours of my day. From probably 5AM to midnight we had every single hour filled. It looked kinda like this:

5:00am – wake up/get ready
6:00am – workout
7:00am – workout
8:00am – school
9:00am – school
10:00am – school
11:00am – school
12:00noon – lunch (at school)
1:00pm – school
2:00pm – school
3:00pm – school
4:00pm – practice #1
5:00pm – practice #1
6:00pm – practice #2
7:00pm – practice #2
8:00pm – practice #2
9:00pm – home, shower, dinner
10:00pm – practice orchestra?/homework
11:00pm – homework
12:00midnight – homework/bed

In building this diagram of my schedule, Kendra first asked me to list the things that were unmovable in my day. I think that after that we were supposed to add in more negotiable activities. But from Round 1, we recognized an issue. There were quite a few other things I would have liked to add to the list, but they genuinely weren't much of a reality in my actual daily schedule, so we kept it real. We only laid out the things that I routinely did every day. In doing this, we realized that if my day consists of all the things it normally does, the only time that you could consider "free time" in my 20 hour day might have been found in the 15-20 minute car rides to and from locations.

In evaluating this schedule diagram, we realized how impossible it would be for me to devote time to any other things that I wanted or felt called to do. There is not a lot I have figured out about life now, let alone then, but what I knew for sure was that the most important things I could be doing with my time and energy were loving God and loving people.

Now my written schedule has never included an hour set aside and titled "love people," but somehow it happened. In the classroom, on the wrestling mat, at my lunch table, and in the car with friends were all prime time for honoring the people around me and making them feel encouraged and appreciated. Not only was loving people in the midst of my busyness sufficient, it was pretty much ideal for the relationships I had at the time.

I can't say the same was true about my relationship with God, though. I wanted to know Him better, hear from Him more often, and experience Him in a more intimate way. I wanted and needed to spend time with Him...and surprisingly, it's rather difficult to have a constructive, intimate, two-way conversation with anyone (God included) while you're taking notes in class, wrestling, surrounded by your friends at lunch, etc.

Yes, there were times that spending time with my people needed a designated spot on my calendar and yes, I did sometimes wish that I could have had more spots set aside for that purpose. But, for the most part, bonding and intentionally growing together was embedded in all the activities. My growing closer to the Lord, on the other hand, required me to spend consistent one-on-one time with Him. I knew what I needed to do. But how? When? I had created a schedule for myself that was too full to include the One who created me. *Red flag.* And if I didn't have time for something so important to me, what other things of significance were I missing out on simply because of my busyness?

I didn't have to let life completely have control over me.

One thing for sure, I made Kendra's work cut out for her. This wasn't an easy problem to solve (which is why I so gracefully poked over it until she made me face it). Truth was, life this way wouldn't be sustainable forever. But it was my current reality. I mean, I could not rationally just mark off an hour designated to school and reassign it to time with my friends. Nor could I just decide to go spend an hour alone with the Lord instead going to wrestling practice (though more days than not, I would have HAPPILY made that transaction). Still, I didn't have to let life completely have control over me. Kendra explained that it is in my purpose and design to have control over it. We then went into the significance of having margin in our schedules (and the absence of it, in my case).

KENDRA

The summer before Kenya's junior year she was involved in everything under the sun, and she had more opportunities coming her way. From what I could see, she wasn't quite overwhelmed yet, but there was a growing amount on her plate. A common result of people who are high capacity is that because they are so gifted and talented, everyone wants them to be a part of their initiative, on their team, or on their committee. Kenya, being the ten-talent kid that she was, had a high demand on her time and a high demand for her attention. However, everyone who wants you on their *team* is not necessarily part of your *dream*. And the ability to determine when to say no is one that needs to be learned at a young age. So on one of our Sundays during church, we went into a room with a white board and I had her write out her weekly schedule from 5:00 a.m. to midnight, 7 days a week. I thought that she was on the path to running herself ragged, but in her mind she was being productive by getting stuff done. I

Everyone who wants you on their team is not necessarily part of your dream.

58

think it was helpful for her to see the visual snapshot of what her weekly schedule looked like.

To her credit, in that season she really wanted to work on consistently spending time with the Lord. But with the workload of AP classes, wrestling, serving at church, early mornings and late nights for wrestling, she was finding it difficult to set aside time consistently. So as we looked at her schedule, I really wanted her to understand not only what it means to have margin in her schedule, but also how to have a schedule full of the right things.

In the book *Present over Perfect*, Shauna Niequist gave me the language for this principle. Many of our teenagers are growing up in an age where we have told them they can do anything they put their mind to, and we have flooded them with opportunity. While this is good, there may be other consequences. The pressure that is put on them regarding their performance in school, family, friends, and work creates varying levels of stress. As a result, the National Institute of Mental Health reports that in 2016 suicide was the second leading cause of death for teenagers.

So before life got even more complicated, I wanted Kenya to learn the importance of being intentional with her time and her schedule. First, if you pre-determine what the priorities are in a particular season, it makes it easier to say no to the things you *should* say no to. With adulthood on the horizon, I also wanted Kenya to be able to recognize what her priorities for her life were and what others' priorities for her life were. Most teenagers are going to have adults determine much of their daily schedules, and that is understandable. However, as teenagers transition into more and more freedom and into adulthood, they have more and more control over their time.

Kenya had already earned her parents' trust and was starting to have more choice and control over her time. If she did not learn to be intentional, then the possibility of other people filling her time instead of her filling her time could become a reality. As adults, we see this all the time. Have you ever gotten through a day, a week, or a year and you look back and remember being extremely busy, but you felt like you did not get anything done? Chances are it is because your time was spent tending to other people's priorities for you instead of tending to your own priorities.

For Kenya, in this season, a priority would be time with the Lord. Instead of committing to getting to it at some point in the day, she needed to pre-determine when it needed to happen and then fill in things of lesser priority around it. Remember, our values and priorities can be found in the pages of our calendar.

Just because you can do it all does not mean you should do it all.

Second, I wanted to communicate the importance of having margin in our schedules. If every moment is planned, if there is no wiggle room, then where is there room for the spontaneous? Where is the room for the fun things that may pop up? Just because you *can* do it all does not mean you *should* do it all. Now as wise as this sounds, the truth is that I was learning this lesson with her. My strengths lean towards planning and logistics. I am the one who has my day, week, and month fairly planned out. However, in this season, the Lord was teaching me to make room. Not necessarily for something specific like attending church on Sunday or serving throughout the week—those things were already happening, but with seemingly every moment of every day planned, I felt like I was missing out on the random things that God wanted me to do. I did not want the ship to run so tightly that we were in so much of a hurry and on a schedule that we could not find God in the mundane or take time to pause and slow down when He asked us to.

What You Say No to Determines What You Say Yes To
For those of us who have decided to pour into our teenagers, the phrase "time management" does not always convey all of what they need. As you do life together, there are multiple principles that can help teens determine what they should be saying yes and no to. First, they need to learn to prioritize. Perhaps you have seen the illustration of how someone fits the sand and big rocks into the jar. The trick is that you have to put the big rocks in first, then fill in with the sand around them. The same goes for us. Make sure you have accounted for the big and important things in life. Once you do this, the small things seem to find their place. There are few things worse than not being able to commit to something or someone you would like to commit to because you have already

committed to something or someone to which you did not want to. This is why it is important to know what your "yeses" are.

Second, there needs to be a healthy rhythm between "doing" and "being." Notice I did not say balance. Balance implies that the goal is to always get the scales of life to be 50/50. This is not realistic. There will be busy seasons and seasons of rest and recovery. Our teenagers need to be able to discern which type of season they are in. Going 100 mph all of the time is simply asking for burn out—body, mind, and spirit. There are times to go hard and "be on that grind," but treating life as if we have no limits is irresponsible. Going 100 mph must also meet the season where you refuel the car, perform maintenance, and prepare to go again. We should absolutely capitalize on our time, talents, and gifts. Sitting on the couch all of the time and not using what we have for the Kingdom does not glorify the Father either. As you see your teenager go about life, use the concept of rhythm to help them identify what kind of season they are in, so they can learn to recognize it on their own.

Chapter 6 Reflection Questions:

1. Is your teenager over-scheduled with activities?
2. Of all of the things they are involved in, what do they love to do?
3. Where is the breathing room in their daily schedule?
4. Where is the breathing room in their weekly schedule?
5. How do you model rest for your teenager?

Chapter 7

SHOW UP FOR THINGS THAT MATTER

"Just show up, as you are. You don't have to look or feel great. You don't have to be prepared for each challenge or know all the hows of every situation. You don't have to be fearless, or have all the answers, or be 100% ready. Nobody is any of these things. Nobody ever was. It's not about being perfect, at all. You just have to show up, as you are, despite all the objections and insecurities of your mind, despite each and every fear that threatens to hold you back, despite the limitation and criticism others will place on you...This is your life, your journey, your adventure, and all it's asking of you is to show up for it, as you are. That's enough. That's more than enough. That's everything."

~Scott Stabile

May 2017, End of Kenya's 11th grade year
The Street is Two-Way

KENDRA

In May of 2017 I bought my first house. As a young adult, now with a house and my first full time job, I felt as if milestones were being checked off the list. It felt as if I were passing markers of adulthood.

While I usually pass most milestones with little fanfare, this one felt different. I am notorious for marching on to the next goal instead of celebrating a victory. In addition to the financial commitment of buying a house, this felt like a big deal. It was important to me. After I had signed the papers and gotten the keys there was only one thing I really wanted to do. I wanted to sit in the moment with my people.

Thinking about it now, it was a "disciples who make disciples" moment. I wanted to share that moment with the person who was discipling me and the person I was discipling. Kenya and my mentor Jen came over and the three of us prayed over the house and walked the property line before I moved in.

I imagine I looked like I knew what I was doing way more than I actually did, but Jen was the one who actually knew what was happening. Even though I was learning in the moment, I wanted to show Kenya what it looks like to set the spiritual tone. Having known very little about those who were in the house before me, I wanted to be sure there was a line in the sand drawn. As we prayed around the house, I intentionally walked the property line. Declaring peace over every inch of the property. Praying that it would be a place of peace not only for me, but for every person who would step foot on it.

This would include not only Kenya, but many of her Kingdom Family and friends. I knew that huddling around the bonfire in the back yard many nights and making s'mores was soon to come. I wanted her to know what kind of place I wanted that home to be and to see what it meant to set aside and declare the house for ministry as well.

This right here was one of the bedrock principles of our relationship. Just come do life with me. There are many ways to develop someone, but this is the one I chose. Partly because it's how Jesus did it, but partly because I think showing and telling together has a powerful effect.

I wish I could find more words than "it was a big deal" to describe that day, but as the person who always tries to show up for other people, it was incredibly meaningful to have someone show up for me. I am not always good at communicating to the people closest to me what I need from them and I somehow expect them to read my mind, which is never realistic.

I thoroughly believe in the power of prayer and declaring battle lines in the name of the Lord. Hear me clearly, nothing was going to be in that house or on that property before it was prayed over. However, I look back on that day and feel the swell of gratefulness that my people showed up for me. As I remember it, I had not given them a lot of notice. Jen had a life of her own including three kids, a husband, dogs, and farm animals galore. Kenya, one of the world's busiest teenagers, also found the time. It felt like a mini miracle to me to be able to get them to the house at the same time.

A week later, Kenya blocked off her entire day to spend it with me and my parents as we shopped for bed sets, couches, and bookcases. Getting time on her calendar by her junior year was getting difficult, so for her to block off an entire day still blows my mind.

Now, this may come as a shock to you, but I do not love shopping. I would rather not do it. So having Kenya accompany me while we were being accosted by sales reps in furniture stores made the entire day more enjoyable. I basically have Kenya to thank for there being furniture in my house.

KENYA

I very vividly remember the day that Jen, Kendra, and I went to pray over the house. I think it was because it was something so foreign to me. I mean, it made sense, to pray over the place ...we don't know its history, Kendra is going to LIVE there, ministry is going to take place there, heck I'm going to be there plenty (especially since there is a fire pit for s'mores in the back) and I'd also like to feel security and peace while I'm there.

But I had never done anything exactly like that before. I compared it in my head most closely to when I would pray over the sanctuary while it was still empty. I would pray for the butts that would make the cold seats warm and the hearts of the people who owned those butts. I would pray the enemy far and the Spirit near. I still managed to work myself up about it, however, thinking about what to do, what words to say, etc.

When it came down to it though, the details of what I prayed, what parts of the property I did or did not walk, whatever the heck Jen was doing with the oil, and all that jazz, was of little concern to Kendra. Yes, she wanted her house prayed for and we showed up to do that. But in my mere participation of this whole shindig, I got the great opportunity to do what Kendra had never failed at doing for me. I got to show up for her when it mattered.

To this day, I am pretty sure Kendra has never directly asked me to do anything else or be anywhere else and portrayed it as significant to her. Her priority is always me. And though, I think I very rarely verbally ask her to show up, she just knows when it is important.

Not too long after Jen and I prayed over Kendra's empty home, we had to fill it with stuff. To make it a little less empty, we started with the big stuff like furniture. I remember Kendra mentioning on several occasions how much she was dreading this process terribly. Though I have never owned or filled a home of my own, I absolutely love furniture shopping. It is like fun fantasy shopping for me. So when I offered to come help whenever the day came, I did not think much of it other than, "Kendra hates this and thinks she is bad at it, I like it and think I am good at it....my help sounds valuable here." Apparently it was.

The furniture outing was the first time I got to meet Kendra's family. Boy, did a lot of things about that woman make sense after getting to spend some time with them. I drove my beat up 1998 Toyota Avalon with no AC and mildewed carpet and we followed her parents around all of Knoxville, from furniture store to furniture store. I could not tell you what we talked about alone in the car (probably nothing since the windows were down so that we could breathe) nor in the stores. I do know that even though we spent hours in stores with the help of dozens of sales reps, there were very few major decisions made that day.

I followed like a puppy and aimlessly wandered off every once in a while. I got distracted by random things that Kendra would never really need in her house. I shared my opinion pretty much only when it was asked and even so, I'm not sure how much weight it really had against Mr. and Mrs. Berry (ha-ha). So when, at the end of the long day, Kendra had very clearly and deliberately shared her appreciation for my being there, I didn't quite get why at first. I wasn't all the help I'd made myself out to be.

It dawned on me later though, that again, it wasn't what I had to offer in regard to furniture that Kendra appreciated. It was just me. Showing up. Us. Doing the things together. And it made perfect sense.

> *It makes all the things worth it, knowing that the people you love care enough to show*

I never appreciated Kendra's presence at any of my wrestling tournaments because she had knowledge to help me on the mat. I didn't appreciate her showing up to the award ceremonies because I needed to hear the extra applause in the audience. There is something that happens in your heart when you know, in the back of your mind, that your people are there for you. It makes all the things worth it, knowing that the people you love care enough to show up.

April 2018, Kenya's Senior Year
Signing Day

KENDRA

In high school, it felt like Kenya was a part of every extracurricular known to man. From church, to sports, to school, and her community she was deeply ingrained in so much. There was no way that I could show up to *every* event, game, meeting, or awards ceremony. That wasn't possible. Kenya was the teenager I was called to in this season, but I also had three godkids under the age of ten in Knoxville, and a niece and nephew in Virginia that I was going to stand before the Lord and be accountable for. So even though I couldn't be at everything, I communicated something to Kenya very directly. If it's important to you, you need to tell me so I can get it on my calendar as soon as possible. I had no problem making her a priority. I fought hard to do so often. However, it's hard to prioritize something that you don't know exists.

Remember that the priorities of our lives are shown on the pages of our calendars and the details of our bank statements. If you want to know what is important to you, check where you spend your time and where you spend your money. I wanted to be sure that if it was important to her it became important to me. The same way she showed up for me when I bought the house, I wanted to be sure that I showed up for her.

All of that sounds extremely thorough and well thought out doesn't it? I am a person who loves to have a plan. What I frequently did not factor in was Kenya's tendency to not let me know events going on in her world until the absolute possible last minute. Enter again one of our fundamental personality differences. My need to plan every detail. And her need not to.

Now, a few years down the road in some time of reflection I am able to rationally process and remember a few things. One, Kenya is one of the most gifted, brilliant, loving people I have ever met, but she still makes mistakes. Two, if I had to juggle her schedule and life as a teenager, I probably would have missed a few things in there also. The amount of details she had to remember was extensive. Three, as the adult in our early relationship, I had much more practice with juggling life than she did...and I needed to give her some grace.

This all sounds great now. I promise you that every time she had plans change at the last minute, or I realized that my plans were about to change at the last minute because her plans had changed...let's just say on a good day I was frustrated and on a bad day I wanted to strangle her.

This was no more apparent than when Kenya participated in her collegiate signing day. This is the day that student-athletes have a celebration of their high school careers and sign their letters of intent to play for the college of their choosing. Now if you are not an athlete, let me explain it to you: this is a big deal. This is potentially the culminating event of your high school sports career. For most sports, your senior season is over and senior night is complete. Graduation is about a month away and this ceremony puts a finishing book end to your high school career. Where athletics is full of training, getting better, and being disciplined, this is an intentional moment where you get to celebrate.

Kenya went 87-0 and won her state championship four times in high school and was headed to wrestle in college. So we indeed had a lot to celebrate. This was not one of the smaller ceremonies or recognitions of her senior year. This was one of the top three. Her family was so gracious in inviting me to most events that I felt comfortable showing up to everything and it was no longer a surprise when we were all there to support or celebrate Kenya.

So when she tells me the day before and starts with "Please don't be mad," I could only begin to imagine where this conversation was about to go. Now, as I've said, Kenya had a pattern. So my mind was already thinking that she needed to move something the two of us were going to do or maybe she had won another award she had not told me about. "Uh-huh, ok," I told her, as I tried to steel myself to knowing my schedule was about to change in some shape or form.

"Signing Day is tomorrow," she says. And I remember thinking, feeling, and doing many things in that moment. I'm not exactly sure how, but I remember sighing and being silent at the same time. Trying to make sure that, on the spectrum between frustrated and wanting to strangle her, I am not going to say words I regret. In the same moment, I check my calendar and see what we can do to make it happen. I know that I cannot show up for everything, but this was a pretty important thing.

Luckily for me, there was nothing on the calendar that could not be moved that day. I showed up to Signing Day in the appropriate school colors and just marveled in watching Kenya getting to celebrate years and years of hard work and discipline. Not only that, I walked away in awe of the community of people who showed up for her that day. She had invested a great deal into wrestling over the years and that was the primary reason we were there, but she had also invested a great deal into people, and this was evident.

I still shake my head thinking about how frequently she double-booked herself, or how she forgot to tell me something that I really probably needed to know. However, reflecting back on that morning in her high school auditorium, I remember how many of her people showed up to celebrate, love, and support her. Parents, siblings, grandparents, teammates, friends. She had a mini-crowd. The Facebook post I made about it says it best.

Kendra's FB Post:
Today was fun :) The one thing I don't talk about enough regarding Kenya is how hard she works. Most know how well she reflects Jesus, loves others, and fights for the Kingdom...but she also works harder than any teenager I know. Doesn't matter what it is. She will not be outworked. Her work ethic goes without comparison. Is she crazy blessed? Yes. Does the amount of favor make sense? No. But she has stewarded well what she has been given. I call her a ten-talent kid because she was given five and she has used her gifts and abilities, so the Kingdom gets double in return and people are loved well. Lots of HVA students left early to get to class on time this morning. Her squad stayed. It says something when those closest to you, who love and respect you the most, simply show up. WHO comes before DO and her DO is an overflow of her WHO. Let the good times roll sis :)

Show Up For Things That Matter

This principle garnered two stories because the principle itself needs little explanation. To develop and win the heart of your teenager, show up for the things that matter. In order to do this you have to know what things matter—to them and to you. As adults we have lives and your teenager is most likely not the only relationship you are trying to develop. Have a conversation. Be intentional. Be strategic so you make the "can't miss" events.

> *To develop and win the heart of your teenager, show up for the things that matter.*

Second, be present when you are there. Be proactive so you can be 100% present once you arrive. Do not show up to the ball game and have to check emails the entire time. Don't show up to the recital mentally rehearsing your presentation for the next day. Showing up means showing up. Body, mind, soul, attention. Be present so you can absorb and retain details. Notice how much joy your teenager gets from doing their thing. Connect the dots of how hard they have worked and the outcome that it resulted in. If you are going to show up, show up fully.

Lastly, be flexible. Life changes. Plans change. If flexibility is difficult for you then buckle up for the teenage years. Even the most well-organized teenagers are still learning. They are learning how to navigate multiple commitments and multiple relationships. If you recall, your march towards adulthood was not without bumps. Do your absolute best to roll with the punches.

When the time happens that you cannot show up (when, not if) for something that matters, it will not be nearly as catastrophic if you have made a routine out of doing your best getting there when it counts. We are human and it is important for our teenagers to see that side of us as well. Besides, the fact that we are human allows God to be who He says He is.

Chapter 7 Reflection Questions:

1. What activities are important to your teenager?
2. What activities are important to you?
3. Are you present for different types of activities?
4. What do conversations look like when you can't make things that are important?

_____

_____

_____

_____

_____

_____

_____

_____

_____

_____

_____

_____

_____

_____

_____

_____

Chapter 8

GOD IS WHO HE SAYS HE IS

"Stay on the path, because you don't know
what lies ahead of you. Because you're not
God. All He asks you and I is to put one foot
in front of another."

~*Rich Wilkerson Jr.*

**Summer 2017, Summer before Kenya's senior
year**
*Either we believe what we say about God or we
don't.*

KENYA

My senior year of high school, as you can imagine, was
full of tedious planning and big decision making. I'd say

that the biggest decision that I have made to date was made in the second semester of my senior year: where to go to college. Where to assign the next 4+ years of my life to. Choosing what place would lay the foundation for my future career. Thinking about what my long-term goals and dreams for wrestling would look like and trying to decipher what programs/coaches would support them best. Deciding how close or far and therefore how often or how scarcely I would get to see my family. Navigating how much debt I wanted and would be prepared to handle for the years following college. There was so much. To say that I was overwhelmed with this one decision might be a slight understatement. Truly, I felt rather consumed by it. Life was still happening. Monday through Friday I still had to go to school and wrestling practice. On top of regular life, I had several meetings each week with my academic counselors at school. My weekends were filling with out-of-town visits to prospective schools. At any given moment, I had a minimum of ten tabs open on my laptop of different school websites, research about women's collegiate wrestling, unopened emails from coaches or admissions counselors or scholarship foundations or whatever else.

It had become very important for me to make good, God-honoring decisions, and this whole college thing seemed like a vital step in my life now and for the future, which put even more stress on choosing wisely. I wanted to ensure that whatever college I chose would align with what God would have chosen for me. I thought I understood what it meant to surrender a choice or process to God and that's what I wanted...His will, not mine. I was fully prepared and willing to take my feelings and opinions out of the equation and follow full speed ahead in the direction He wanted me to go. The issue was, I COULDN'T FIGURE OUT WHERE HE WANTED ME TO GO!!! I prayed. And I sought wise counsel. And I prayed. And I read scripture. And I prayed. And I sought wise counsel. And I prayed. Over and over I did the things I knew to do to align my heart and mind with God's so that I could discern what He wanted for me. I just wanted to make the right decision.

I'm not sure how much Kendra picked up on how this decision weighed on my heart and mind, but somewhere along the way she helped make the weight feel a lot less heavy. Once again, she took me back to the student ministry offices in our church building, a place where we'd both become quite comfortable. I'm not exactly sure how the conversation began, but somewhere early on she drew three sloppy red rectangles near the bottom of the white board and proceeded to tell me that they were doors.

So I'm looking at three "doors" and she asks me which one is the right one.

"The right one for what?"

"Which door is the right door to walk through? Which one has the prize behind it?"

"Kendra. I don't know. That's not fair. How am I supposed to know what's behind each door?"

To which she pretty much explained that that was exactly her point. I can't see behind any of the doors. But she challenged me to question whether it was outside of the realm of possibility for all of the doors to be good to walk through. Why couldn't there be a prize behind all of the doors? She explained to me that God isn't holding His hand over one door (or one decision) and waiting for me to choose that specific door so that He can bless me. God finds joy in blessing His children. And after all, He is all powerful. Why couldn't there be a blessing behind each door? Even if the decision I were to make didn't include the best circumstances or wasn't the best decision I could have made for myself by the world's standards...there is nothing that counts God out of blessing even a poor decision. HE'S GOD!!!

Why couldn't there be a blessing behind each door?

What I took away from this is that regardless of what decision I made for college, God could bless it. My job is simple: surrender and honor. I had to surrender the decision (which was a heart posture I strived for) and to honor Him with whatever decision was made (which I also fully intended to do). After checking these two boxes, the only thing left to do is pick a door, run through full speed, and watch the blessings flow. Not saying that this will be with complete ease or be absent of trials, hiccups, or strife. But even through those things, God is who He says He is. Holding on to that truth in the midst, and in the aftermath, of all decisions is what keeps you on track to receive the blessing.

Having this understanding under my belt truly freed my heart for the remainder of my college search. It wasn't much later after this conversation that I went to visit just another prospective school on the list that ended up being my final choice. Being there, I had so much peace. I liked the school. Things made sense financially. So I made a decision. Was it the "right" one? Why couldn't it be? I knew that I was going into it with God on my side. And let me tell you, almost two years into that decision, He has blessed my socks off through it. It has been the absolute perfect place for me. I was sent friends that will last a lifetime, professors who care and invest in me personally, a wrestling program that I strive in, and all of the things I could have thought to ask for.

What attests to what I've learned about the power and goodness of God is that He could have sent me all of these things regardless of what school I chose to go to. I don't believe I made the "right" decision. I didn't necessarily choose the correct door. I just chose to take God with me through whatever door I was going to walk through and not to my surprise, I found Him to be faithful.

The doors analogy has been one of the most beneficial lessons I've learned and is one that I have shared numerous times with friends (or strangers even) feeling burdened with the weight of making a good decision.

KENDRA

Going into Kenya's senior year, she still had not made a decision about where she wanted to go to college. Some of the best college programs for women's wrestling were recruiting her. As someone who values education, but was also a collegiate student-athlete, believe you me, I had a lot of opinions. However, I recognized that she had to go through her own process, and I tried to wait to give my opinion until it was asked.

This was an important place for me to check my experiences at the door. There were many points where my college athlete experience was, let's say...rocky at best...and as I saw my sister begin to step into that world, I was nervous. However, there were a few things I reminded myself of to keep me at bay. One, my experience was not going to be her experience. Our sports are different. Our coaches are different. The culture of our teams are different. The schools are different. And the two of us are different.

I will be the first to admit that she left home a mentally stronger person and had already competed at a much higher level than I had when I left for college. I received quite a shock when I got to college about the level of training and commitment it would require to excel. Kenya already had a foot in that world, and she was much more prepared.

So when we sat down at the white board that had served us well over the years, the goal was to be able to inject some peace into Kenya's decision-making process. She did have a lot of factors to consider including tuition, wrestling programs, academic programs, and she even had an option to attend college out of the country! Think back to when it was time for you to make decisions at 18—ones that you knew would impact the rest of your life. It can be stressful. And I had seen the weight of making a good decision start to get to her.

Looking back, I may have even directly or indirectly contributed to some of this stress because one of my mantras for teenagers is the importance of good decision making. I feel like Kenya understood this, but I had not done a good job of explaining the other side. Decisions are important, and I lean towards making decisions with all of the relevant information. While this can be a good thing, particularly to grasp in teenage years, it can also be hurtful when it leads to "analysis paralysis."

If you are not familiar with the phrase, I imagine that you may recognize the concept. Analysis paralysis occurs when you are considering all of the factors and information so much so that it actually paralyzes you from making any decision; good or bad, correct or incorrect.

When you are circling every angle of a solution and shining lights on contingency factors and thinking through ramifications so much so that you do not make a call. When there is so much information that you cannot see a way forward, you just keep circling the problem instead of making decisive steps towards a solution: that is analysis paralysis.

So we sat down at the white board and I tried to explain using a picture of three doors, side by side, labeled 1, 2, and 3. I said "Kenya, here are three doors. Which door is the prize behind?" So of course she is looking at me a little confused and trying to figure out where I am going with this. Eventually she comes up with "I don't know," which to her credit, is the logical and correct answer. I mean, would you be able to make any more than a random guess? I tried to press her a little. "Are you sure? I mean, it's pretty important to get it right. Which door is the prize behind?" By this point, we both know that there is a question behind the question and a point that I imagine she hopes that I would make sooner rather than later.

Moving things along, I ask the same question with slightly different wording "Ok, we have three doors. Which door is the blessing behind?" It is the same question, but I wanted her to start thinking on a bigger scale. Kenya probably politely endured me trying to drive home the point she did not quite understand yet, so after a while I just got right to it.

I explained to her that we serve the God who spoke the stars into existence. The God of the universe. So would it be impossible for there to be a prize behind each door? Would it be inconceivable that our God is so in control and loves us so much that there could be a blessing behind each door? Could it be that you have a ton of great options for college? And while you are desperately trying to make the right decision (i.e. choose the right door), the reality is that God is big enough to bless whatever decision you make (i.e. make every door good).

The truth is that *Whom* she was taking through the door had much more impact on the outcome than which door she was choosing. No matter which opportunity she chose, her attitude and effort were going to have a tremendous impact on the final outcome—both of which she could control.

God Is Who He Says He Is

By the time your teenager is making big decisions, I hope that you have enough equity in the relationship to be able to speak into them. As we help our teenagers navigate those big decisions, there are a few things we can encourage them to do. First, encourage them to do their homework. They need to research what they are looking into. This can include online research, talking to people who are more knowledgeable, asking the right questions, and observing the environment. What we want to do is not continue to spoon feed them the answers, but teach them how to go find them on their own. What this does is give them confidence and belief that they can find the answers on their own. Remember, they will not be by our sides forever. Are we helping them grow up where they can thrive in the world on their own?

Two, you want to encourage them to seek wise counsel, and keep in mind that means other people in addition to you. The best thing I did for Kenya in her process was take a step back. As she sought wise counsel, I encouraged her to seek out people who loved God and loved her. I knew that I was not the only person who fit that criteria. The Bible says there is safety in a multitude of counselors. She needed people who had different viewpoints and experiences than I did to speak into her.

Lastly, once conversations have been had and information has been gathered, after the Lord's heart and will have been sought and there is nothing else to do but make a decision, remind your teenager that God is who He says He is. The pressure this generation feels on a consistent basis is through the roof. For them to be reminded that the universe and their universe is not solely dependent upon them can help relieve some pressure. I am not saying that you downplay the importance of the decision, rather I am saying that you magnify the greatness of God.

For those of us who have put our faith in Jesus, sometimes we need to be reminded that God is who He says He is. I can only imagine God looking at us and shaking His head as we go about our lives concerned with every detail and worried about every decision. We declare all the "omnis" on a Sunday morning; omnipotent (all powerful), omnipresent (everywhere), and omniscient (all knowing). However, we tend to forget to move those Sunday declarations to the rest of our week and the rest of our lives.

I am not saying that you downplay the importance of the decision, rather I am saying that you magnify the greatness of God.

This was what I wanted to bring back to the forefront as I walked Kenya through her decision. Worst case scenario, let's say you make the wrong decision. There are three doors and you choose the wrong door. God is big enough to bless your wrong decision. Think about it. We are so worried we will make the wrong decision, but we serve the God who created the stars. He spoke and things appeared. It is not too farfetched to believe that he has the ability to help us course-correct.

He did it all throughout the Bible. That does not mean we are absolved from doing due diligence or seeking His heart, but what I knew about Kenya is that she was going about it the right way. The reality is that there are often multiple paths to end up in the same destination. For all we knew, all three doors could have gotten her to where she wanted to go. She had gathered all of the necessary information. She had weighed the pros and cons. She had sought the wise counsel of those around her. She had prayed through it and asked Jesus for guidance. At that point, it was time to pick a door and walk confidently through it.

Chapter 8 Reflection Questions:

1. In what areas is it difficult for your teenager to trust God?
2. How could you start a conversation about this with your teenager?
3. Do you model trusting God with decisions and other things that are hard for you?

Chapter 9

IT'S ALL ABOUT PEOPLE

"Love is greater than power."

~*Danielle Strickland*

October 2017, Kenya's Senior Year
Love God. Love People.

KENDRA
I cried the whole year.

As we were firmly into the fall of Kenya's senior year, she still hadn't made a decision about where she was going to college. As people began to ask her, she didn't really have an answer. In circles of high school seniors and conversations, people were starting to talk about possibilities and maybes. Kenya wanted no part in these conversations. She is a bubbly happy person who is open and honest in conversation, so when she completely shut down conversations about the future, I knew that she was not ready.

It wasn't only in social settings where she would skirt around the answer and briefly mention that she was still deciding. Even when it was only us one-on-one, she politely but quite emphatically, did not want to talk about it.

Honestly, this was a big issue for me. While I could understand why she did not want to engage in those conversations, the problem was that I needed to start the very long process of realizing that we were approaching a new season. In less than 12 months, the most consistent person in my day-to-day life, the person that I had poured so much of myself into the past five years was not only not going to be in the same city, but most likely not in the same state, and quite possibly not in the same country!

Change was coming and time was not slowing down. I was ready to start processing out loud by August. With her senior year starting, I believed that if I talked about and verbally processed the change that was coming (whether good, bad, or indifferent) that by the time she graduated the following May I would be prepared.

By the way, I was wrong. May rolled around and the tears were still flowing.

A change in seasons for Kenya marked a change in so many things other than physical location for the two of us. The best way I could describe our relationship was that we simply did life together. Most of the principles in this book were not a "come meet me at Starbucks and we are going to talk about the principle of showing up for the people you love." Most things were taught from doing life together. And somewhere in there the benefit of how much time we spent together began to compound.

A potential physical move for Kenya meant that not only would I not get to spend as much time with her, but also that our relationship was going to shift. We had developed such a great rhythm that I was not eager for this to happen. I knew that I would start having to view and treat her as an adult. Now granted, a young adult, but it was a shift that was going to have to take place nonetheless. I imagine that it is similar to what parents have to go through at some point when they move from a parenting role to an advisory role in the life of their kids.

Lastly, Kenya leaving for college left me asking "Is she ready?" Have we taught her everything that she needs for the real world? Does she have the life skills she needs to be successful? Does she have a handle on time management, on having to make a tough choice, on having difficult conversations? Is she ready?

All of these were ideas I would think about when I thought of Kenya going to college, but none compare to the one single thought that so easily brought tears to my eyes no matter where we were and no matter what we were doing.

I was going to miss her...a lot.

So by August, I desperately needed to start saying words out loud to be able to process that the rhythm which we had built was about to change significantly. The problem though, was that she was not ready. We had reached an impasse. She was not ready to say words out loud and I needed to say words out loud.

After a few false starts with me trying to get her to talk about it, I had to realize that she was not ready and me forcing it was not going to help. So I found a solution in the middle. I started processing on my own by writing letters to her to get all of my words out of me...and didn't give them to her. A perfect solution? Probably not. However, as I started to use keystrokes to express all of my emotions, she continued to march towards making a decision about college.

October 14, 2017 – Letter #1
All of a sudden it hit me...it's the last fall I'm gonna have with you. And at that point the tears had welled, up but it got worse as I started thinking of all the lasts. The last Rise Up, Christmas, Christmas break, Fusion, high school wrestling...and I had a complete meltdown while driving... between the summer and fall I threw you a few softballs and even fastballs to see if we were going to even

acknowledge the fact that it's your senior year and to put it out there that, at the very least, some things will change between us. And while you're pretty even keel on most things this one was an automatic no go. You were not talking about it…

Earlier this week Pastor Jeff said something that stuck with me. Success does not happen without succession. So as the two of us go into some of our lasts together, I'll be honest. I feel like my window is closing. I'll be the one to stand accountable before God when he asks what I did to love you, equip you, pray for you, encourage you, lead you. And to be honest, I'll be accountable for that with multiple people, but it's you that I'm paranoid about having to get it right.

October 28, 2017 - Letter #2
We haven't really talked about your Rise Up messages since you did them. I got to listen to the 2nd half of your breakout when you did it for the high school girls. It is without a doubt the best I have seen you speak. You seemed comfortable. And that says a lot and comes through when you speak. I still remember you sending me your outline and even though it wasn't completely together in your head yet, I could tell that you put an extreme amount of effort into it.

Any time you speak, I struggle because my brain wants to do multiple things. One, the student in me wants to take notes. Girl. You can teach. And it's GOOD. Two, I just want to soak up watching you do your thing. I just wanna watch you go. These moments are special, and I feel like I've got to grab them when I can.

I'll stand by what I said, you were different this time. I really think you were Holy Spirit-led. Yes, you were comfortable and yes, you were prepared, but the Spirit is the difference. Don't forget that. That goes for multiple parts of life.

So we marched on through her senior year. And I'll tell you, it was a year to behold. I'm just shaking my head thinking about all of the events, stories, and awards we chose not to expand on. We would be here forever. What is particularly noteworthy is when she broke into my house over Christmas break to decorate while I was out of town. Also, there was this small thing in February where she won her fourth state championship. However as February rolled into March, we started to get to the good stuff. The stuff that would last forever.

March 2018, Kenya's Senior Year
The Whole Point

KENYA
Kenya's FB post:
"This. This is the moment I've prayed for relentlessly. This is why God pursues us relentlessly ...so He can have us forever (insert mixed skin tone praise hands emoji here).

Hey best friend, I'm proud of you. I'm excited to spend eternity with you (pink cheeks, smiley face emoji) But until then ...let's walk this journey together. Love you."

A lot went down senior year. The most remarkable moment for me, though, had to have been the night I got to dunk my best friend. It was the night after Wednesday night Easter service, 2018.

Leading up to this, you need some context to understand why this was significant to me. Obviously, my buddy punching her ticket to eternity had a great deal to do with it... but there's more to the story.

I met Kylie my junior year of high school in speech class. I noticed her. She stood out from all the people around her, pretty much all the time. I remember all of her speeches fully captivating everyone in the room in our nine-week course. She radiated joy and oozed energy every time that I saw her. It was easy to see that she had quite the personality, but for whatever reason I deeply wanted to know what Kylie was like beyond the surface. From just a few conversations we had and things I'd picked up on her saying, I gathered that Kylie was not a Christian and that bothered me. It provided even more motivation to get to know and actively love on this girl I barely knew.

To this day, I remember the confused, disgusted look on Kylie's face when I called her over to me while we were doing some in class research in the library to tell her,

"We're going to be friends." I'm 100% sure she thought I was crazy. Still yet, we became friends. It started with small talk in the cafeteria and eventually led up to me picking her up from her house every Wednesday night to come to church with me. I prayed for Kylie with a heavy and believing heart. I was more intentional with my words and actions towards her than I'd been with anyone else in my circle. I wanted her to see Jesus so badly, and I knew that likely the only consistent presence of His she saw was inside of me. I needed her to know that she was created by Him, loved by Him, and wanted by Him. So I did everything in my power to spark conversations, hoping she'd bring her questions about God, and hoping I could use my actions to show her His love.

It was probably a year into our Wednesday night church routine when Kylie and some other friends came to an Easter service. There was nothing particularly special about the message or the worship experience, but I think that night we saw the fruit of a culmination of things for Kylie. I vividly remember her telling me she wanted to understand more about baptism. I freaked. "Hold on one sec. Let me go find someone who knows more about this stuff than I do."

Within a matter of minutes I was sitting in a conference room with Kylie, another one of our close friends and two adult leaders. We were talking about what it means to be a child of God. By the end of the convo, Kylie said that she wanted to carry that title. So with big smiles and full hearts, we headed to the baptismal pool.

KENDRA

As much fun as I had with Kenya and as much as the focus has been on wining and developing her heart, the hope has also been that she has picked up on what I was doing. By her senior year we had come quite a way in the friend department. From sitting on the field at Johnson University begging the Lord to bring her the right people, the Lord had more than shown up. By the time she was well into her senior year, she had found her squad.

So as the Jesus in her began to spill out and onto her friends, they started coming to our student ministry with her and I got to know them pretty well. Very few words describe what we do well in our student ministry, but 'intentionality' is one of those words. For two years I watched Kenya be the hands and feet of Jesus to her friends. I watched her not beat them over the head with the Bible but speak Truth and show grace. She kept at it and continued to seek Jesus to get ahold of the hearts of her friends.

There are only a handful of times when Kenya was somber, quiet, melancholy, or sad. The times that I do remember her in those demeanors were when it was a question whether the people closest to her did not know Jesus. She very clearly understood that people's eternities were in the balance.

Looking back through my social media, I still remember the seriousness and then the joy of this day. The weight of someone's salvation...well that's what led to the joy of them meeting Jesus and then the celebrating once they came out of baptismal waters.

Watching Kenya go after the heart of her friends—it's hard to describe what that felt like. I do know that it was the ultimate example of how life is all about people.

Kendra's FB post:
It was about 8:50pm. "Technically" service was over, and we had finished baptisms. But we serve a God who exists outside of time. And over 2,000 years ago he watched his Son die a brutal death so we could be with Him forever. And last night He didn't care how long it took. I imagine Him being outside that door saying "Take your time. This is too important. I'll wait. You see this...this is the entire point. Nothing is more important in this moment."

And like Micah said...when you have teenagers who carry their friends to the feet of Jesus and show the love of the Father...that RELENTLESS and RECKLESS love and pursuit...yea we celebrate! Kylie is gonna be with us forever!!!!!

Love God. Love People.
The expectations surrounding our teenagers is so incredibly high. I should know, I am the first to hold the people close to me to high expectations. High expectations are not necessarily a bad thing, but as Andy

Stanley says, "Memorable is portable." There are so many things that I want our teenagers to remember, but after they know who they are, it boils down to love God and love people. That is the expectation.

The sub points are numerous, and we talk about a few of them in this book, but if our teenagers can develop a consistent life of loving God and loving people, they are going to be ok.

Love God – So much of what we want our teenagers to do starts with having a healthy perspective of who God is. A. W. Tozer says the most important thing about you is what you think about God. Jesus said, "If you love me, you'll keep my commandments." Loving God and loving the things of God over time translates to loving what God loves and caring about what God cares about. This is how you align your heart and your desires with God's.

"Love God" also succinctly covers the first five commandments (Exodus 20:3-12):
No other gods, only me.
No other gods; of any size, shape, or form of anything
No using the name of God, your God, in curses or silly banter.
Observe the Sabbath day, to keep it holy.
Honor your father and mother.

Love People – The Bible says, "By this everyone will know that you are my disciples, if you love one another." I always think of how many options that Jesus could have used for people to understand that we are His. He could have said by how you pray, by how you serve, by how you sacrifice, by how you memorize scripture, or by how you build ministries. He could have picked from any of these options, but instead he said "by how you love one another. That is how people will know you are my disciples." It is the outward demonstration of an inner decision.

"Love God" and "Love People" are good anchors to have.

"Love People" also succinctly covers the second five commandments (Exodus 20:13-17)
No murder.
No adultery.
No stealing.
No lies about your neighbor.
Don't set your heart on anything that is your neighbor's.

When the world gets complicated and our teenagers feel like they are drowning under the weight and the stress of expectations of life "Love God" and "Love People" are good anchors to have.

Chapter 9 Reflection Questions:

1. How does your teenager intentionally put God first in their life?
2. How does your teenager intentionally put other people before themselves?
3. Is there somewhere you could volunteer or serve together?
4. How do you model putting God first?
5. How do you model putting other people first?

_____

_____

_____

_____

_____

_____

_____

_____

_____

_____

_____

_____

Part II

Chapter 10

YOU REAP WHAT YOU SOW

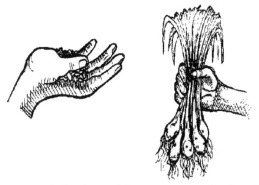

"Some of the best things we can do for the kids in our lives is let them sit in the consequences of their successes or failures."

~*Tim Elmore*

April 2018, Kenya's Senior Year
She got it.

KENYA

Our student ministry senior dinner was a night that I was soooo looking forward to. Low-key because it was going to be for me. Don't get me wrong, I loved serving the friends and family in my ministry. But there was something particularly exciting about getting to show up to an event, an event of celebration, and have zero responsibilities. The only thing I had to do was enjoy my family, enjoy my friends, enjoy the grilled chicken and buttered rolls, and sit back and reminisce. Oh, and I was asked to speak for a brief moment. I was a bit nervous, but that didn't feel like a chore. I was so excited. I was honored that they wanted me of all the seniors in our ministry. And I was pumped about the opportunity to share, with hundreds of people in the room. FpStudents meant a lot to me; it was far more than a filler activity for my Wednesday night schedule.

I and about eight other seniors took turns trying to muster the words of what FpStudents meant to us. Most people talked about community. That was big for me too. One of the biggest revelations I had of God's provision was how He gave me a family in Faith Promise when I needed it. Other people brought up the significance of what they had learned in their years there. I sure learned a lot too. About God, about myself, about leadership, about everything. But what I could not leave that stage without relaying was how the people in that room helped me to discover my reason for being on this planet. What I am most indebted to in that ministry and the people God sent me through it (primarily Kendra of course...who I strangely hadn't seen much of that day) is my coming to understand my purpose. What I know now that I wouldn't have otherwise is that my life is not just about making a good life for myself. It's not about arriving, making money, having a family, being happy, and leaving. They taught me that I am a part of something so much bigger. My life is about living a life I am specifically called to: loving God, keeping my eyes on heaven and helping as many people to get there as I can along the way. I learned that I have a reason for being here that is outside of myself. I have a purpose bigger than me.

After sharing on stage, I finished eating with my parents. Eventually, we had a time where all of our families would pray over us. The staff and volunteers in the room would roam around and lay their hands on their kids as well. My head was down, I heard words...but I never knew who exactly was praying over me at what times.

I stayed after to help tear down: stack chairs, take down the table settings, vacuum crumbs off of the ground. Kendra was there too. Other than the brief photo shoot we had at the end of the event and the quick "I'm proud of you" before my time at the mic, this is the first time I'd really seen her at all that night. I remember seeing her in the back when I was speaking on stage, away from our people. I remember thinking about how proud she must have been. The things that I was saying, that I was thanking our ministry for teaching me, these were the things I know she worked so hard to instill in my heart and mind. These were the topics that filled our lunch dates and late-night conversations. These were the things we prayed about together.

Purpose. Eternity. Calling. These are the things that matter. Kendra taught me that.

KENDRA

Every year in our student ministry we would hold a dinner for the high school seniors and their families. Now this would be classified as our annual "fancy" event. As dressed up as we were going to be in student ministry, with dresses, shirts, ties, and dress shoes, we celebrated. Our worship center that seats over 1,000 was transformed into tables and chairs that sat eight to ten per table and included a photo booth for us to document the affair. It was a beautiful time as seniors and their families from not just our campus but from every campus filed in.

Most years, this was one of the student ministry events for which I was all in. For the students and families that stay through senior year, you get to know them and their stories well. Watch them mature from the awkward middle school years to confidently taking on the world. It's one of the benefits we get to reap from pouring ourselves into the next generation. I love seeing everyone from all of the campuses, I love the spirit the evening has as we serve our families, speak a blessing over them and celebrate. It's fun to be part of that experience.

However, Kenya's senior dinner was a little different for me. My first instinct related to anything in our student ministry is to jump in and help, but not this time. I had the incredible blessing to walk through just about every phase of Kenya and student ministry. It was the home base of our relationship. Not school and her grades or sports and wrestling. It was church where we met, grew our relationship, and sealed our friendship. So that night I made a strategic personal decision. I decided that this night would be for her parents.

I did not need a recap of what she had walked through and learned in our student ministry. I was there. From the lock-in events, to the times she spoke on the platform, to when she ran her own serving team, I got to be there for each of those moments. This was her parents' time to celebrate. So contrary to everything else I did with Kenya that year, I hung back. I did not sit at her table. I did not interact a lot.

I have to admit that I did act a little selfishly. You see, by not being at the table and not making eye contact with Kenya for most of the evening, it meant that she would not be able to see the tears that I could not stop. This was an extension of the "Kendra cried all year" scenario. This was yet another culminating event for her, and a clear delineation of the end of a season, for her and for us.

As everyone wrapped up eating, we moved into the program. They had a panel of seniors come up on stage and answer this question, "What has FpStudents meant to you?" Now I tell you, this was a sight to behold. I looked up on stage and as I looked, I had a relationship with 90% of our kids up there. Most had started at our campus and had then moved to other campuses, but we stayed in touch, connected through social media, and every time we had an event where we pulled everyone together I got to see them, catch up, and hug them tight.

Two out of the three seniors I was responsible for that year were on the stage, and it was such a sweet moment. I got to sigh, breathe deeply, and see a visual representation of why some of us chose to pour ourselves into next generation ministry. The cream of our crop was on the stage. Teenagers who loved, and served, and prayed, and worshipped. These were those kids. And while the question was "What has FpStudents meant to you?", the unspoken question that I heard was "Did we do it right?"

The microphone was passed down from one teenager to the next. My other senior on stage took the microphone. I don't remember everything he said but I do remember how he talked about community. About how he found his. How it is important to have one. He talked about his small group. Talked about the brotherhood they had. Talked about what his church family meant to him.

Mind you, I am standing in the back still crying, but these are tears of joy. These are "thank you Jesus" tears. We are not a perfect student ministry, but this is one of the things we want them to walk away with. Our 2018 word of the year as a ministry had been *Family*. He walked away feeling the importance of family and knowing that he had one with us. I could hardly stand it.

Kenya gets the microphone in her beautiful navy-blue dress, looking like every bit of the adult she is about to step into. I remember I sat down, preparing to take in every word that I could. It was hard to hear through my tears, but she talked about family and stepping into purpose. And the more and more she spoke the more and more I was jumping up and down inside because all I could think about was "she got it."

I can still see myself shaking my head in the back. We do not get everything right in our student ministry and I am not a perfect person, but I'll tell you this, I love Kenya Sloan. And for most of the time we spent together, there was no grand plan. This book has been about some of the things that were important along the way, but the overall strategy was "I love you. Let's spend time together." That was it.

And to hear her get up and talk about the Kingdom family she has at church and how we had equipped her to step into her purpose...these are words from the 18-year-old you've poured everything into.

Well, by this point, I'm about blind with tears so of course it is time to move on to my favorite part of the program. As we celebrate and congratulate our seniors, one of the last things we do is pray over them. This is awesome, except it is in direct contradiction to my strategy for that evening: let her family have this moment and don't let Kenya see the rivers coming out of my eyes.

So as we start to pray and have parents pray over their kids, I walk away from Kenya and her family. Can't start there. Way too much emotion. As staff and small group leaders walk around the room, laying hands on and praying for seniors, I join them in moving from table to table, praying over and speaking blessings and protection over the kids to whom we have been entrusted with for the last seven years.

I made a circle around the worship center. Grateful that there was time set aside to pray over our kids and 100% avoiding the kid I needed to pray over most. However, as I began to circle back towards Kenya's table, it became inevitable. Eventually it was time for me to go lay hands on my baby sister and pray protection and purpose over her. I don't remember what I said, but I remember it feeling like I prayed heaven down.

Interestingly enough, as I reflect on that very holy moment, I remember that I did accomplish my goal. No eye contact with Kenya so she couldn't see the tears. I think it's funny that I felt like that was a priority. Like she hadn't seen me cry all year.

As the evening wrapped up, I exited sobbing mode and we took pictures by the photo booth and helped clean up once everyone left. It was a culminating moment, but it was still April. We still had a month until graduation and then the summer before she left for college. And I planned to enjoy every single moment.

You Reap What You Sow

All of Kenya's senior year, and that night in particular, was a time of reaping what we had sown. That is where a lot of my tears were coming from, because I was getting to reap the benefits of pouring my life into someone for six years. Now in the grand scheme of life, I know many of you are reading this thinking "six years, that's nothing!", and I would probably agree with you. I still have a ways to go to be faithful with something or someone for decades. However, for young adult me, that was the longest I had done something of significance other than sports or school with that much intentionality for that long of a period of time.

As Kenya and I walked through life together, it was not only me who taught her about sticking with something. Sports did. Do you want to reap championships and wins on the mat? Then you have to sow in 6:00 a.m. workouts and a diet that does not make sense and a discipline that most teenagers never see.

When we walked through decisions, she learned to think through them with this principle in mind. What are the consequences of this decision going to be? If this is what I choose to reap, what am I going to have to sow? This is a biblical principle and it is seen more than once throughout the Bible. The verse that comes to mind the most is Galatians 6:7 "Do not be deceived. God cannot be mocked. A man reaps what he sows." 2 Corinthians 9:6 says, "Remember this: whoever sows sparingly will also reap sparingly, and whoever sows generously will reap generously."

There is no coincidence that opportunity and blessing followed Kenya in high school. A lot of it is because she sowed hard work and discipline into the things she chose to invest her time in. She also chose to sow love and sacrifice into the people she cared for the most. It is not a coincidence. It is a biblical principle. There are many times where we have to be strategic. Decisions are not always easy. There are tradeoffs in life. Sometimes it is a choice between a bad option and a worse option, or a good option and a great option. Sometimes it is a decision between a good option and a God option.

Kenya is great, but she is not perfect. As she chose to be strategic at times, she was not always on the fun side of you reap what you sow. Sometimes she chose to sow into time with friends over studying and reaped the outcome in her grades. Sometimes she chose to sow into staying up too late knowing that an early morning practice was coming, and she reaped the consequences of being tired and sluggish at practice. Sometimes she chose not to sow into writing things down or leaving herself reminders and had to reap the consequences of having to backtrack once she double booked herself or forgetting she was supposed to be somewhere.

However, while she was not perfect, I can say this about Kenya. Rarely was she surprised of the consequences. Nine times out of ten she would weigh the pros and cons of decisions and choose what she was able to live with, despite the consequences. And she was ready to face them head on.

> *If we do not teach the teenagers we love that there are consequences to their actions, it is a reflection on us before it is a reflection on them.*

If we do not teach the teenagers we love that there are consequences to their actions, it is a reflection on *us* before it is a reflection on *them*. We reap what we sow. And as the adults who love them, it is our job to teach them this.

Chapter 10 Reflection Questions:

1. Does your teenager take ownership for their successes and failures?
2. Does someone often rescue them from tough situations?
3. How can you encourage ownership of decisions and actions?
4. Do you model taking ownership for your successes and failures?

_____

_____

_____

_____

_____

_____

_____

_____

_____

_____

_____

_____

_____

_____

Chapter 11

TRAIN EM UP, SEND EM OUT

"We have got to find the balance between gather and go."

~*Jonathan Haskell*

June 2018, Summer after Kenya's senior year
Time Is a Changin'

As spring rolled into summer, I tried to make sure I was being more intentional about forcing myself to recognize that Kenya was indeed crossing into adulthood. I began to recognize that where it had been easy to convince her of most things, there were some decisions I was going to have to let her make on her own. There had been little advice that she was not receptive to over the course of our relationship. Even if she disagreed, she would normally hear me out and at least give me the satisfaction of appearing that she was listening. Not this time.

That summer she was picking her classes for her freshman year. We were at a Young Adult Groups event at Maple Street Biscuit Company. Who doesn't love biscuits?! I was excited because we had made a strategic push to get the high school seniors to this event. This was one of the transitions that I could get excited about because while most of the transitions during her senior year marked the end of a season, this event reminded me that we were both in the young adult season. Granted, she was fresh into "young adult" having turned 18 months before and I...well...let's just say I had been in young adult season for more than a decade at that point.

As we were hanging outside and milling about, I gravitated towards the high school seniors and Kenya's group of friends. I have always been more comfortable with teenagers than with my peers, and this was no different. After all, these were Kenya's friends. I had just spent a great deal of time with this group, particularly over the last year.

The conversation turned towards the future. Kenya and a friend started talking about college classes and what they wanted to take in the fall. I smiled, was ready to hear their thoughts and provide some feedback. I had a stake in this conversation. Not only because Kenya was processing through important class decisions for herself, but because

I had some experience to contribute to this conversation. Or so I thought.

After Kenya's friend ran through her plan as she went the nursing route, Kenya started talking about her plans and let's just say I had very strong opinions. Not what she was taking, but how much.

I brought four years of being a student-athlete to the conversation. Additionally, I worked for four years as an academic advisor for college students...specifically for student-athletes. This was my wheelhouse. I lived and breathed this environment for eight years and one of those years, I was a freshman student-athlete myself. I was speaking from experience, not what I randomly thought.

Having been a former collegiate athlete and having been extremely challenged by my freshman year fall term, I knew that her taking more than a full load of classes was not a good idea. There was a very clear pattern that I had seen living in collegiate student athlete world for eight years. Every freshman struggles to some degree. I have seen it happen with walk-ons, the star recruits, and everyone in between. It does not matter how good of an athlete or how good of a student they are, there is a natural transition that happens for every freshman student-athlete. Adjusting to the increased freedom that comes with college, multiple workouts a day, going from the top of the totem pole as a high school senior to the bottom as a college freshman and being away from home are all thrown into an equation to equal a simple output: freshman year in college as a student-athlete is hard.

So as academic advisers, the way we typically helped combat the transition effect was to have them take a lighter academic load their freshman year fall term if at all possible. Take one less class (fewer credit hours) to help create a buffer for a successful, healthy adjustment. The transition would still be difficult. I took one less class during the fall semester my freshman year, but still struggled through college Calculus at 8:00 a.m. and wanted to walk away after three weeks. Shout out to Jeff and Lori Holtfreter for offering a safe place and saving the day!

There were very few things where Kenya and I flat out disagreed, but this was one of them. We did not scream and create a dramatic scene outside Maple Street Biscuit Company, but we were surrounded by her friends who were very interested in our disagreement. I remember trying to explain all of this to her from my "wealth" of experience and how taking more than a full academic load was not a good idea. Remember, no matter how talented one is, freshman year fall term is an adjustment for everyone.

A little longer into our back and forth than I would like to admit, I realized that this would be one where she would have to learn by experience. I wanted to protect her from being over committed. I wanted to protect her from feeling overwhelmed. I wanted to help her ease into her new rhythm of college athlete life. But the reality was that she was an adult, and I needed to realize that this was not the hill to die on.

...this would be one where she would have to learn bv

Almost a year later, as we were talking about writing this book, this disagreement came up and as we reflected on it, Kenya helped me see exactly why it had been so awkward. I had thought that it was because we did not disagree often, but I learned from Kenya that it was really because I had violated one of the principles I had been trying to instill in her. I had been in the wrong. Not with trying to give her good advice, but how I did it, the environment we were in, and how I would not let it go in the moment.

I was in the wrong because for the last seven years of our relationship and for every moment since then I have been trying to teach, convince, and remind her that who she is, is more important than what she does. In that tense moment, I had communicated that school and grades were the most important thing. Important enough to get into a back and forth in front of her friends at a church event where we were supposed to be hanging out and building relationships. Yikes!

After all these years, even though she was an excellent student, school had never been the primary focus of our relationship. So why was I trying to make it in that moment? Was it important? Yes. Was it the most important? Absolutely not.

Train 'Em Up

What I learned on that beautiful summer day is something that every adult connected to an eighteen-year-old has to keep in mind. At the end of the day, they will eventually have to go. Now believe you me, I hated even typing those words. If we steward the time we have with our teenagers well, then they will be ready (as much as they can be) to step into the world; to make their own decisions, good and bad, and leave their mark. All of the training, the teaching, the advising, the role modeling...we do it because eventually we will not have the opportunity to do it in the same way that we have before. We have got to train them up in order to send them out.

That includes letting them make their own mistakes. Think back, how else did you learn some lessons? I remember my parents explicitly telling me one thing, ignoring their years of experience, and believing that I knew better anyway. It's ironic how I recognize that process now. That is simply a part of it. It is a part of growing up. Making mistakes and course correcting is how many of us got to where we currently are.

The need to protect them from the world stifles the very process in which they can learn to grow and flourish. It is important to recognize that for the teenagers we love, it is not enough to merely "get them to 18." While 18 and high school graduation is a milestone, there are other questions that need to be answered. First, are they ready?

For some of our teenagers, being alive and seeing 18 is itself a miracle and something which they and you are very proud of. However, "Are they ready for the next season of life?" is a valid question.

Second, what is staying the same? In the midst of transition, possibly leaving home, gaining more freedom and responsibility, what supports are still in place for them to lean on? Not to use as a crutch—pulling the rug out from under people is rarely successful in my experience—but to continue to aid them on their journey. At the very least, have you taught them what supports they need to set up in their next season? It may be a life change, but some things (friends, discipline, faith, etc.) are going to be needed no matter what season of life they are in.

Lastly, whether this is asked directly or indirectly, out loud or implied, our teenagers are asking "Are you still with me?" I do not mean physically. So many of our teenagers will no longer be in the house with us or in the regular rhythms of life as we have come to know them, but they want to know "Are you still with me?" Do you still have my back? Can I still come to you for questions? Are you still in my corner? Are you still on my team?

Situations are different for every relationship, but my prayer is that you have the opportunity to not only say yes, but communicate it through your actions more over time. During high school I rearranged small parts of my life to communicate to Kenya that she was a priority, and this did not change when she went to college. Perhaps what I rearranged changed, but she was always a priority. The response to "Hey, do you have a sec to chat?" text messages that I would get from her was always yes. If I did not have a second, then I would create one.

Visiting her in Kentucky, making sure I was free when she came home to visit, letting her know specifically how I was praying for her. None of this was done in a bubble, because even though she had been trained up and sent out, I wanted to communicate that she knew I was still here for her. That our relationship did not stop because she went to college. I am in it for the long haul.

And particularly with us being slightly over 10 years apart in age, quite honestly I am thinking long term not just for her, but for me as well. When I close my eyes and think about my future and my family, I see Kenya being a godmother to my kids one day. I see her as one of my closest friends. Inner circle kind of close.

You're stuck with me, sis!

July 2018, Summer after Kenya's senior year
Before Kenya leaves for college

KENYA
So there's this place. It's called Max Patch. It is a major landmark section of the Appalachian Trail that is found

on the border between Tennessee and North Carolina. It's beautiful. And when I say beautiful, I mean BEAUTIFUL!!! At one of the mountains' peak, there is this little plateau. When standing on this plateau, you have a full 360 view of these wonderfully crafted mountain ranges and valleys. I'd only ever seen pictures, but I'd wanted to visit for some time now so that I could sit and revel in the beauty for real. The thing is, I didn't want to go to Max Patch at just any time of day. I'd seen the most beautiful pictures there as the sun rises from beneath the mountains and lands itself comfortably above them in the sky.

All this to say, when Kendra told me we were going, I was stoked. I also hadn't done the math. She tends to think of these types of things before I ever do. In order for us to make the two-hour trek with no chance of missing the sunrise, we'd have to leave Knoxville by 4:00 a.m. This is how I knew she loved me. Neither of us would consider ourselves morning people and this was more than just morning. To me, 4:00am is still very much nighttime. I got to sleep in the car though.

We went, we saw, it was beautiful. Kendra said it was a little cloudy to see the sunrise. I wouldn't know the difference; it was all just pretty to me. Eventually she said she wanted to find a "spot" in which, when found, we sat down and she handed me an envelope. The envelope had my name written small and plain in the center. Inside was a letter, also with my name written at the top of it. I knew immediately what I was holding. This was my "goodbye letter."

She had much to say, as you could imagine. But there were three main points about my identity...surprise!!!

1) "You are a Woman of God."
2) "You are a Warrior."
3) "You are a Worshipper."

Now I know that me moving away to college didn't mean that Kendra and I were never going to see each other again, but it did mean that things were going to change between us in a way. We both clearly understood that. The letter was less of a goodbye and more of a summation, a reminder of the things she'd emphasized over the years, since she would no longer be able to remind me in the day-to-day cadence we'd gotten used to. Of all the things we'd learned, experienced, and talked about, the most important things she could relay in this moment were things about my identity.

After she explained in detail these three aspects of my identity, she relayed that she had just one request.
"One day you're gonna meet someone and you'll get the nod from the Holy Spirit that they are the person you'll need to pour into...Disciples making disciples is not just a catchy phrase. We are mandated."
There was a lot more in the letter. It still means a lot to me. I keep it in a grey box that I take out often so that I can be reminded of who I am and why I'm here. Like

Kendra so gracefully put in the introduction of this letter, "the most important voice [I] need to learn to hear is God's, but sometimes He sends people to help communicate to us what He is saying." He speaks to me loud, clear, and often through Kendra's words...and not just the ones written in my letter.

After we left our spot, we headed back to the car. As I was getting in my seat, I noticed a cute little Pandora bag with a purple ribbon tied around it. Kendra had found a way to sneak it in there when I wasn't looking. In it lay a simple brown bracelet with three silver "W"s on it, standing for "Woman of God," "Warrior," and "Worshipper." I am really picky about the jewelry that I wear so the fact that she'd found something that I actually liked said a lot. But also, I love it because I get to wear it on my wrist as well as in my heart. Pretty cool things happen when people ask me about it too.

I was much better company on the trip back to Knoxville. We stopped for breakfast at this tiny, locally owned country restaurant on the way home. It was a good day.

KENDRA
That summer Kenya was crazy busy as usual. The combination of training for wrestling, checking the final things off the list to prepare to go to college, and spending as much time with her friends as she could manage had her all over the place. However, I wanted us to have some time too. As much as I tried to slow down time, I had been

unsuccessful. She would leave for school in the coming weeks and time felt like water: hard to hold.

I am frequently reminded how much I love Kenya by small things. Namely, that I give her the aisle seat in church, but on this particular day it was because I chose to wake up at 3:30 in the morning for her. I am telling you, the list is small of how many people I would happily do this for.

For a mini-graduation trip, I asked her what she wanted to do and eventually we settled on watching the sunrise at Max Patch in the mountains. Great idea. I love the mountains. The only thing was that the mountains were a couple of hours away, which meant that in order to be there for sunrise, we would have to leave before sunrise. Very very early. After the 3:30 wake up call, by 4:00 we were off and rolling towards the mountains.

After weaving my way up the dark backroads where GPS is no longer helpful, we eventually pulled up next to other cars pulled off on the side of the road. Eureka! We were in the right place! We gathered all our blankets, backpacks and snacks and headed down the half- mile path to get through the woods to the clearing.

As we are gathered with the pockets of other people waiting for the sun to come up, you can look around and just tell it is going to be beautiful. We are in a clearing that gives you just about a 360-degree view of the mountains around you. Breathtaking would be an understatement.

Being outside and in nature is something that is a highlight for Kenya and myself, but a beautiful view was not the only goal of the trip. Seeing as this may be one of, if not my last moments with Kenya before she embarked on her new season, I wanted to make sure that she had an anchor. I wanted to try and communicate one more time a few of the principles and lessons we had been talking about for the last few years.

Mentors, parents, coaches, and teachers have done this so many different ways over the years; trying to create this capstone moment. I wanted her to take away concepts, but I also wanted her to have something tangible. Now in case you have not picked up on this, I have a lot to say. So just to be sure I didn't miss anything, I wrote her a letter.

This letter had been years in the making. What in the world do I say now? Of all the things I could say, what should I?

So after we watched the sun rise, explored and took pictures, we came down from the clearing and found a spot away from everyone. I gave her the letter to read and while she read, I closed my eyes and tried to do some combination of pray over her and not cry. You can imagine how well this worked out, so eventually I stopped trying.

Once she finished reading, neither of us really had too much to say. I'm sure that I hugged her and then back down the mountain we went. I also wanted her to have something tangible to help remember, so we had one more surprise once we got back to the car. A bracelet to solidify everything I had just told her. A visual reminder of who she is.

Send 'Em Out

It took me a few weeks to write that letter. Eventually I began to understand that at that point all I could do was reinforce what I had already told her. This was not the time for new information. If I was going to tell her anything that was going to stick, it needed to align with what I had been telling her for years. Better yet, I knew that my words should serve as reinforcement to the actions that I had consistently showed over time.

> *I knew that my words should serve as reinforcement to the actions that I had consistently showed over time.*

So while all the details of what I told her were only for her, as I look over that letter there were three components that every teenager can benefit from.

1) Tell them who they are
2) Tell them you love them
3) Tell them what you want them to do

Tell them who they are – Of all the things I could have written about, this was the pinnacle. The cool thing is that it lines up with one of the core principles. Who you are is more important than what you do. So I wanted to focus on who she was. The foundation of our relationship is Jesus, and the Kingdom, and the Church and so as I reminded her of who she was. That is where the focus was. Not on her grades, even though she was a great student. Not on sports, even though she was an incredible athlete. Not on all the awards, even though she had to be the most decorated senior on the planet. None of that, absolutely none of it, compares to who God created her to be. And I wanted to make sure she knew it.

Tell them you love them – More than anything else, I hope she read the letter with a "duh, Kendra" going through her mind. This one more so than the other two. Please do not let your capstone moment be the first time you have expressed "I love you" to your teenager, whether it be in words or actions. I so desperately hoped that when she was reading what I wrote that it was so deep down in her that it was something she already knew. It is important, I believe, for us not to leave to chance that our teenagers will understand how much we love them through inference or deduction alone. I wanted her to know fully that I am on Team Kenya and that I love her. I wanted to make sure she knew that I loved her through the actions and words I had said and showed over the years. Like in *Remember the Titans*, I wanted to leave no doubt.

I want to emphasize, if there has not been intention with this until a capstone moment, have the courage to do it anyway. You may fumble, it may be awkward, but those three words "I love you" are the ones that we all need to hear. And if you have a relationship with a teenager and you are having a capstone type of moment, they need to hear it from you. Tell them. If you have never said the words or you have never directly and intentionally communicated it, tell them. Their hearts need to hear it from you.

Tell them what you want them to do – A capstone moment is a great time to leave them with a charge. With everything that is inside of them. With everything you have poured into them. With how much you believe in them. What do you want them to do? And so that is what I told her next. We had been talking about it and using the language the last few years of what I wanted her to go do. It is the last principle.

Chapter 11 Reflection Questions:

1. What have you implicitly or covertly tried to teach your teenager?
2. What have you explicitly or overtly tried to teach your teenager?
3. What few things does your teenager know you believe without question?
4. What ideas or beliefs do you believe your teenager will take into their next season?

_____

_____

_____

_____

_____

_____

_____

_____

_____

_____

_____

_____

_____

Chapter 12

DISCIPLES WHO MAKE DISCIPLES

"Every kid is one caring adult away from being a success story."

~Josh Shipp

February 2019, Kenya's Freshman Year of College
What Stuck

KENDRA

In February of 2019 I got to visit Kenya over a weekend and spend some time with her at college in Kentucky. Most student ministry staff and volunteers really have one goal for a graduating senior in their student ministry: to connect the heart of a teenager to the Kingdom and equip them to own their faith. Kenya was the epitome of the involved kid in student ministry and at one point she led multiple teams within the ministry. I had no doubt that we did all the things while we had her in Knoxville, but as she stepped into adulthood away from the day in and day out culture of our church, and had much more freedom and choices, the question lingered in my mind, "What stuck?"

When I left to drive back to Knoxville after that weekend, I left completely filled up and so grateful. Here are some things that I saw:

**1)	She found her Kingdom Family** – As she was introducing me to her friends and as we spent time together, I knew without a doubt that Kenya had found the people who she considered family. The way they treated her, each other, and those around them. I knew that she had spent time intentionally pouring into people and allowing herself to be poured into. I say all the time that "Kingdom Family is the best family" and she had found hers. And these were not your average college students. They started a college ministry together their freshman year. 18- and 19-year-olds. I was absolutely blown away.

**2)	She was building the Kingdom** – The context in which Kenya and I met was church, but I had tried so hard to make sure she understood the difference between our local church and the entire Kingdom of God. The church is filled with imperfect people and that includes us. However, the Kingdom goes beyond a local church or a geographic region. Jesus came preaching and teaching about the Kingdom. The Kingdom is God's operating system in Heaven and our job is to have Earth operate like Heaven. And in order to do that we have to help bring the Kingdom. I had so hoped that she had developed a heart for the Kingdom, not just our church. She got it.

3) **She was seeking God first** – Kenya and I did a lot of church stuff together which was great, but I wanted to make sure she did not confuse her personal walk with Jesus with all the serving that she did for ministries inside of the church. As someone who is extremely busy, and has many commitments, I was so hoping that she was making her personal relationship with Jesus a priority. And she had. She had developed an intention about growing and spending personal time with the Lord, not just serving in every ministry under the sun. Serving is good, but sometimes we are so busy serving that we are not connecting with our Heavenly Father.

4) **Who she was was still more important than what she did** – I'm not sure if there is anything else I tried to drive home more. I said it. I demonstrated it. I celebrated it. I quoted those words verbatim all the time. I tried not to start conversations with how her grades or other measuring sticks of accomplishments were. Over and over and over again. For the entire time I had known her I tried to make sure she understood that it all starts with identity. Everything. The whole sha-bang. And after not seeing her two to three times a week, and after not living in the same city for a few months. She got it. And she had competition for her attention: wrestling, maintaining honor student-level grades, leading a ministry, and leading a small group. There were plenty of opportunities for her to miss it. But it stuck. And she was much more interested in who she was becoming than what she was doing.

Disciples Who Make Disciples

And lastly, what I saw from that trip was that Kenya had truly embraced the concept of disciples who make disciples. Probably around her sophomore and junior year of high school our church started using the phrase "disciples who make disciples" to succinctly capture Matthew 28:19. It says, "Therefore go and make disciples of all nations, baptizing them in the name of the Father and of the Son and of the Holy Spirit." The essence of that passage talks about how this is one of, if not *the* key thing that those of us who believe in and follow Christ should be doing. I loved it because it was biblical and because it was what my life looked like. I was pouring into Kenya, but there were people pouring into me. It was way more than a catchy phrase or tag line.

The last part of the letter I wrote Kenya and the last part she read when we were in the mountains was that I wanted her to be a disciple who makes disciples. I know that our story did not start with us and I pray that it does not stop with us. There are people who poured into me long before I had poured into Kenya. And my hope and prayer is that there are going to be people who hit the lottery when Kenya decides to pour into them.

Choosing Kenya to pour into was not coincidental or happenstance for me. I knew that she was going to help take back ground for the Kingdom. She's an exceptional person. And I wanted to make sure she understood that what we were doing, the relationship we were building, and the things we were learning did not stop once we drove away from that mountain. She had a responsibility to turn around and pour love, belief, and principles into someone else. And then they would pour into someone else, and then they would pour into someone else. And years down the road we would see that we indeed had made disciples who make disciples.

I had asked Kenya to make this a priority in her life and you could tell that she had. You could tell that she lived life on purpose as she began to pour out the Jesus in her onto and into people. That weekend I could tell, that even though she was still a teenager, she had gotten it. Some of the principles and priorities had stuck.

I drove home from Kentucky that day, sad to leave her. Desperately trying not to cry and lingering past the time I needed to leave. I still missed her. However, I had come to grips with something as soon as she decided where she was going to college. The Kingdom needed her in Kentucky and that was a good thing. She was ready.

December 29, 2019 - Christmas Break

KENDRA

Well, as Kenya and I sit down to write this final chapter at my kitchen table, we have had quite the experience with timing today. As we have gone back and forth for a few months about what stories to tell you, choosing the story for this chapter seemed to be especially difficult. Now, I realize that was because the Lord wanted us to live it out so it would be fresh. Let me tell you about our day.

It is currently the Sunday after Christmas and Kenya is home for the holidays. That means that our typical Sunday rhythm, in part, is back. A few days ago we made plans for church today. 10:00 service, the middle one, with lunch after and the day spent writing and editing this book.

I left the house at about 9:25 a.m. for a 20-minute drive that would put us on the campus of our church right before the early service let out. That way I would arrive early enough to go grab our seats. As I write this, I recognize that there are some things that are different about our rhythm. Things change over time and that is ok.

One of those things is where I sit on Sundays now. Today was not the front row as usual. My Sunday rhythm with a new friend has us sitting somewhere else. Before service I leaned over, and my friend asked me if Kenya was coming since she was trying to decide if we had the right number of seats. I leaned over and told her that she was...and that Kenya would come bustling in about halfway through the first song. About two minutes later, there she was. Standing next to me and me trying to give her the appropriate, self-contained hug.

After service we took our time, said "hi" to friends and then jumped in the car to head to my house. I love this kid, so we are doing home cooked meals today. Cracker Barrel can happen next time. Garlic Parmesan Chicken over noodles with green beans was the plan for lunch and taco soup in the crockpot with cornbread was the plan for dinner. As I worked on the chicken, I had Kenya working on the soup. I was seasoning chicken breast and Kenya was cutting onions. I was adding Italian seasoning to the chicken and she was adding garlic to the soup. This is something else that has changed over time...my ability to cook has drastically improved since I met her.

After the soup was ready to sit in the crock pot and we had eaten lunch, we cleaned up and moseyed over to the couch. I got my laptop out and was ready to write when Kenya asked, "So when is nap time?" Right now sunshine, right now. About three minutes later I took a picture. It really was beautiful. Kenya is asleep on my couch, in the exact same position and laying the same way I sleep on that couch. As she fell asleep, *Do It Again* by Elevation Worship had come on the TV in the background. As I made the following Facebook post I could not help observing how her heart seemed at rest.

Kendra's FB post:
Sunday after church, home cooked meal in her belly, her song on the TV, she's asleep on the couch...this is the Ephesians 3:20 kind of stuff. No better time than when she's home.

I did not need a nap at that moment, but it was very clear that she did. About two hours into this "nap" I was getting restless. I had a decision to make. Wake her up and gently tell her that we should get to work or let her sleep. I decided that we would have plenty of time to work on the book. This extremely hard working, collegiate student-athlete, who has a heart for everybody simply needed space to sit and rest. Who was I to disturb that?

So instead, I put on tennis shoes and went to do something I should have done months ago: rake the leaves in my front yard. The high that day was in the 70s, uncharacteristically warm for December in East Tennessee. About 30 minutes after I started raking leaves, Kenya comes out of my front door and says "Good morning, sunshine" in mid-stretch.

As I got ready to go inside, I just smiled. She looked rested. Fully rested. I remember how important that was because I had been given the same opportunity a week prior...

KENYA

I'm home!!! It's Christmas break and just because of the way my wrestling schedule works out, I'm here for just over a week. After subtracting all the Christmas and family things to be done while I'm here, there are a few things that will be high on my priority list every time I get to be here. One of which is time with my sister. Kendra and I both love each other a lot and don't get to see each other all that often anymore and both of us are quality time junkies. So it's a must, for both of our sanities.

We had a plan ahead of time: Sunday morning, 10:00 church service, lunch at her house, chill on the couch and write until dinner, dinner and then tentative s'mores to be determined by the weather. A day very well spent in my book. It was good also because this will have been the first time Kendra and I would be able to sit down in the same place and work on the book together, which had been needing to happen for some time now.

So after we, and by "we" I mean mostly Kendra, finished cooking lunch, ate, and laughed at the table for a while, we moved over to the couch where I immediately cozied under a blanket and squeezed one of her perfectly sized throw pillows to my chest. I had pretty much just assumed that nap time was on our schedule for the day. It didn't take long for my body to align its plans with my mind. With the Hot Cocoa scented candle that I picked out burning next to me on the coffee table, some of my favorite music playing on TV, one of my favorite humans on the couch across from me (awake, working on her laptop of course) my tummy full and my heart fully at rest, I slept. For a while, apparently.

I woke up a solid two hours later and arose from my slumber feeling like a million bucks. I honestly had no idea I needed the rest so badly. I was thinking we might get a good thirty minutes in before we needed to start working on the book, we had a lot to do and today was the only day we'd get together to work on it. Our time was limited, important, and to be wisely spent.

When I sat up on the couch, Kendra was nowhere in sight, but I could hear a repetitive swooshing sound coming from outside...so I checked it out. That woman was in the front yard raking leaves! My first thought was "why isn't she napping, we were supposed to be napping!" But what came out of my mouth, as I stretched, yawned, and smiled at the same time, was "Good Morning!!!" She smiled back at me and told me to set up some chairs wherever I wanted to write. She moseyed in and we eventually got started on the back porch (until it started to rain at least).

Here is what I came to realize: I thought we were napping because we needed to nap. But really Kendra was letting Kenya nap because Kenya needed to nap. We also needed to write, that didn't change. But she saw that what was good for me in that moment was to rest. She saw fit that I just be for a bit. This is a luxury that I rarely give myself. And I know it was hard. She doesn't get much of me as it is...and the first time in several weeks that she gets me for an extended period, she creates space for me to rest. She knew it was important for my body to catch up, my heart to be still. This concept is something that I know, from years of experience and dialogue, was taught to her by someone who loves her really big.

KENDRA

A week earlier, I had been at the house and on the couch of my sister/mentor. My big sister no longer lives in the same city that I do, so a few days before Christmas I went to go visit her, her husband, my three godkids and the three dogs. In the crazy busy pace of the life I live, there are very few opportunities that I have to shut it all off, very few chances where I do not feel that I am responsible to anyone or for anyone. Even on Christmas break, a few things from work came up that needed to be handled.

When I went to Memphis to spend time with my big sister and family, let me tell you what I did: absolutely nothing. I am talking about the kind of nothing where you do not get out of your pajamas for consecutive days in a row. The kind of nothing that when the 10-year-old is asked about the last time he took a shower, you have to pause and try to remember the last time that YOU took a shower.

I really don't have any other words to describe the situation other than Jen spoils me. Before I even get there, she asks me what I want for dinner while I am there. Not just one meal. All of them. And when I tell you she can cook, man-o-man can she cook! Quality time wrapped in food is my main love language. And I would do just about anything to be at the giant dinner table that my brother-in-law made.

The Sunday I was there, I remember finally coming downstairs after sleeping soundly. I was two or three days into not having to remember what day it was. After I ate breakfast, Jen was spending the day Christmas baking in the kitchen. Cookies, candied popcorn, Oreos dipped in chocolate, and so much more. Now I love love love love my godkids. However, one thing that is undeniable is that the 6-year-old-girl, 4-year-old boy, and 10-year-old boy are not quiet. It is impressive, the decibel level they can achieve sometimes.

As they are running around downstairs, "helping" bake, playing Nintendo Switch, and taking care of dolls, I found myself in one of my classic positions. On the couch, under my favorite blanket at their house. I did not need a nap in the moment, but the reality is that in all places in the world, their house is my safe place. And there more than anywhere, my heart is at rest.

All of my people were there. Jen, Jeremy and the kids. The timing was right. It was Christmas, so I got to turn my work brain off for a while and the focus was spending time with people. Jen was loving me by taking time to cook all the things and make sure my love language was taken care of. In her words...all of my buckets were filled.

That's how I knew that I needed to let Kenya sleep a week later that day on my couch. Because Jen had spent years teaching me what it means for disciples to make disciples. Everything Kenya and I did that Sunday after Christmas. Church, home cooked meal for lunch, nap on the couch, heart at rest. All of those things were the things that Jen taught me because I had done them with her and her family. Over and over and over again. Sunday after Sunday. Meal at the dinner table after meal at the dinner table. Time on the couch under the blanket. Again and again and again.

Jen often refers to Kenya as her spiritual grandchild and she is 100% right. The amount of time Jen spent pouring into me and teaching me principles, those we have written and not written about, are the same things that I turned around and did with Kenya. Jen pours into me. I pour into Kenya. And Kenya is already pouring into other people. It is Matthew 28:19 in action. It is disciples who make disciples.

We hope that they will turn around, when the time is right, and pour into the people around them.

Which lines up so well with mentoring, does it not? If we mentor the teenagers in our lives well, we hope that they will turn around, when the time is right, and pour into the people around them. The teenagers we choose to do life with will eventually be bosses, parents, co-workers and volunteers in our world and communities. Tim Elmore reminds us that we are not just raising kids, but that we are raising the next generation of adults.

The narrative around the next generation is not always full of hope and belief. But I am confident that if we lead well, mentor well, and disciple well, it will make a difference. There is light in the darkness. How incredible it is that we get to be a part of that light!

Chapter 12 Reflection Questions:

1. Is the way you mentor your teenager the way you want them to mentor someone else?
2. Begin with the end in mind. What do you want for your teenager?
3. We should each have someone we are leading and someone who is leading us. Who is currently pouring into you?

_____

_____

_____

_____

_____

_____

_____

_____

_____

_____

_____

_____

_____

_____

Afterword:

THE STORIES BEHIND OUR STORY

...our story does not happen unless a few other stories happen first...

KENYA

Mom – I have a mother who is not only my biggest cheerleader, but likely the biggest cheerleader any person can have. She always has been. Other people even point out to me on a regular basis how proud my mom is to be my mom. They can see it. And that does something inside of me. Knowing that I am one of my mom's greatest pride and joys gives me so much pride and joy. It gives me a reason to strive to be my best in all that I do. To the people reading this book, you can thank my mom for fighting me to eat my veggies, fighting me to brush my hair at least once a week, and fighting me to do my homework. There was much fighting on her behalf to get me this far (I might have been a slightly stubborn child). I came to Kendra prepped for growing and developing, but at the great price of much grey hair on my mother's head. To the woman who got me through some of my best and worst times, thank you for putting us first and loving us real big. Thank you for encouraging my heart. The losses in life feel less devastating and the wins are so much more worth it because I get to share them with you. Thanks for being my biggest cheerleader, mom.

Dad – I don't know where I'd be without my daddy. This man's entire life has been an effort to give my brother and me the best ones possible. He tells us all the time how the two of us coming into this world completely changed his—and I know it didn't have to. I know that he doesn't have to work his butt off to provide the best for us. I know he doesn't have to move mountains to support us in everything that we do. I know he doesn't have to put our desires and dreams in front of his own. But I also know that, because of who he is and how much he loves us, he wouldn't have it any other way. I never question if my dad is proud of me. Not only because he tells me often, but also because I see it in his face and hear it in his voice in all of our encounters. He has high expectations for me, and he is willing to fully exhaust himself and his resources in order to give me what I need to meet those expectations. This is because my dad believes in me more than I believe in me. He'd break down any wall to show me that I can do whatever I set my mind to. I have yet to see another person, in anyone's life, invest so much of themselves into another. Thank you, Dad for making your life all about ours. I'll never stop working to make sure your ROI is high ;)

Jenny – My dad made one of the best decisions of his life when he decided to marry Jennifer Schmid. This woman has bravely stepped into so many rolls for me. She is a best friend when I need it, a wealth of knowledge when I need it, an adventure buddy when I need it, a warm place of safety when I need it, and so much more. She's never scared of my questions or my feelings. She presents me with the rawest version of herself at all times and that is something that simply can't be replaced. She knows how to encourage me when I block everyone out and often whips me right into shape when no one else can see that I need the whipping. I don't have her blood and she didn't have to choose me as her family, but she did and she does...every single day. Jen, you bring something so special and so fresh to my heart and to our family. We wouldn't be the same without you. I stand by what I tell people often when I share your roll in our sweet little dynamic; you are the greatest blessing God has given our family. Thank you for choosing us and changing us for the better.

Keenan – My little brother is my partner in crime. We've gotten into our fair share of trouble together. But, I mean, trouble builds character, right? Right. On a serious note though, a version of Kenya without Keenan would be meek and insecure and have far less joy. She wouldn't be the Kenya that you've read about in these pages. My brother's life has taught me and continues to teach me what it means to let loose, have fun, love deep, express compassion, and to feel and taste the parts of life that so many people only choose to observe from a distance. Thanks for beating me up, keeping my secrets, being my biggest hype man, and teaching me how to be a human with real feelings. My life is so much fuller because of you, Keenan Sloan. I wouldn't want to embark on all its journeys if I thought there was even a chance I wouldn't have you to share it with.

Nanna and Poppie – My grandparents drew a line in the sand for our family that set the stage for me long before I made my appearance on this earth. They thought about me, not knowing my name or what the details of my face might look like, and made conscience decisions to set me up for greatness. They wanted to ensure that their kids and their kids' kids would have opportunities that they never had, and they worked hard and long to pave the way for us. To this day, my Nanna and Poppie will not let us forget how great of an honor it is to be a Sloan. They've created a culture in our family that calls us to stand by and fight alongside each other no matter what. They remind us of the privilege it is to pursue education and they encourage us to obtain as much as possible. Most importantly, they beg the Lord who has blessed our family for generations to continue to do just that. I never doubt if I am covered and protected because I know the authority in which my grandparents tap into when they stand in the gap for me and the rest of their family. Thank you, Nanna and Poppie, for giving me the safety to take risks, pursue my passions, and dream big.

KENDRA

Mom and Dad – If you have not had the privilege of meeting Russell and Dacia Berry, you really are missing out. My mom and dad had the immense task of raising my brother and myself into adulthood. They had such great influence on me that I still catch myself thinking of things they said to us growing up, even when I do not want to. That is influence.

Without a doubt, one of the key principles they instilled deep into me was that you show up for the people you love. Just recently have I figured out the language around it, but the truth is that I was raised in a culture of generosity. Where the expectation was that we give as Jesus gives. Any time I hear this in church world, most people are talking about money. And while money was something I saw my parents give to the church and to people in need, I also saw them give their time. I saw them give a listening ear. I saw them give up a room in our house for someone to live in for months at a time. I saw them make sure a litany of food was available when people came over so their spirit and their belly could be full. I saw them give out encouragement. Lavishly. Over and over until people felt it deep in their bones. I grew up in a culture of generosity and without it, without their story, Kenya and I might not have our story.

Jen Dickson – About two years after I met Kenya, I walked into this Women's Conference at my church. I was much more of a student ministry person than a women's ministry person, so I wasn't exactly comfortable. The evening session got going and the MC got us all quiet so she could pray over us.

Never in my life had I heard someone pray with that much authority. There was no doubt that something about her was different. The next week, I walk into a Bible study and *shut the front door*, the same lady who was praying is teaching the Bible study. After a few months of me trying to hide in the back and at least say "hi" to her every

Thursday night, she gets up on stage and says "I'm not sure who this is for, but I think I'm supposed to be mentoring some people. If that's you, please let me know." As they say, the rest is history.

I showed up on her couch that December, was in her small group that spring, got a key to the house a few years later, and was then asked to be the godmother of her kids. Jen isn't just my mentor. She gave me a family. Every single thing I did with Kenya is because Jen had done it with me at some point first. On the couch in her living room, on the floor in the kitchen, or in the front seat of the suburban, Jen taught me what it means to go and make disciples.

Jen gave me a safe place and she was my safe person. Good or bad day, I knew I could show up, often unannounced, and just be Kendra. Not student ministry Kendra, or professional Kendra, or community Kendra. All the hats I wear can be exhausting and the weight of expectation is crushing at times. But when I crossed the threshold of her house, I only felt two things: Love God and love people.

I am the person I am today because as a 20-something trying to figure out life, Jen, her husband Jeremy, and my godkids Judah, JuliaKate, and Jacoby loved me until there was no doubt that I was loved. Thanks fam. I miss you guys.

Bonus Mom – Denise Dowell is a saint of a woman. In my freshman year of college basketball, our team was recruiting a strong athletic high school guard from Virginia. Candace got to Furman that next year and quickly became my best friend. With a bond that only teammates could have, I began to come home with her on breaks. I remember feeling welcome, at ease, and crazy grateful for all of the home cooked meals (Do you see a pattern here?). Three years later when I graduated college, her mom gave me a key to their house. If you have picked up on anything from this book, the sappy, sentimental stuff is 100% up my alley. It was a beautiful gesture. I cried and I have not left the family since.

After my parents laid the foundation, Denise Dowell is without a doubt the most influential person through my 20s. She gave me a safe place when I needed to escape the pressure of college basketball. She was there for me for every transition decision. Where do I go to grad school? Do I get another degree after grad school? Do I look for a job? Where do I look for a job? Do I stay in this job? Do I buy a house? Can I do foster care?

The same way I sat there and begged God to bring Kenya the right people all those years ago, I know that my godmother did that for me. How do I know, you ask? Because as I am at her dining room table, visiting her and my godfather for Father's Day, she has been on her knees in the living room praying out loud for the last 45 minutes.

And I'm not talking about "Lord, help us have a good day." I'm talking about begging God to move on behalf of our family and the church. I am listening to her go one by one through family members by name. Eventually she gets to me. I hear her thanking God for me and how He has brought us together. I hear her thanking God for the friendship I have with her daughter. I hear her praying for my future spouse and for my future kids. And I hear her thanking God for the people He has brought into my life in many different areas. How He has blessed me with friends who I love and care about and who love and care about me.

My second mom is a praying woman. And before I knew the power of a perfectly timed well-cooked meal and what it means to have a safe place and what it means to be truly wanted and accepted, she taught me all of those things, because she loved me so incredibly well.

Dave and Tonja – On the hardest day of my young adult life, I came to your house and ate wings at your kitchen table and then went upstairs to purge all of my emotions. You didn't ask questions or try to fix it. You simply told me your door was open. You two have always been a safe place for me and so many others. I'm grateful.

Jenn Borovy – Here is to many more years at the lake and in the woods. You were the first person who pushed me to write a book and when you said I could do it, I believed you. Hear me. I believe in you. Your turn.

Thank You

This book would not have happened unless some people who love us a whole lot decided to pitch in and help out with their time and talents.

<u>Many Thanks!</u>

Ashley Moody

Zac Stephens

Lakyn Basham

Kylie Bowman

Contact Information

Do you have a passion for developing people?
Do you believe mentoring well matters?
Do you believe in serving the next generation?
We would love to connect with you!

Website
canwegotolunch.com

Email
canwegotolunch@gmail.com

Social Media
Twitter: @canwegotolunch
Facebook: Can We Go To Lunch?
Instagram: @can_we_go_to_lunch

Lightning Source UK Ltd.
Milton Keynes UK
UKHW022148090223
416682UK00016B/2225